# Big Rigs

## The Complete History of the American Semi Truck

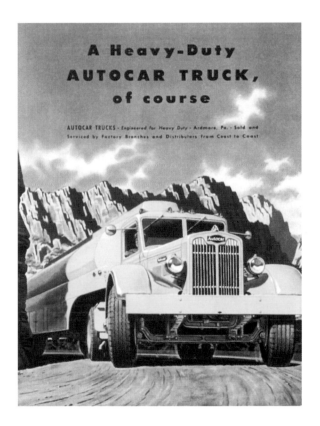

A Heavy-Duty **AUTOCAR TRUCK,** of course

AUTOCAR TRUCKS - Engineered for Heavy Duty - Ardmore, Pa. - Sold and Serviced by Factory Branches and Distributors from Coast to Coast

*Text and photography by*
*Stan Holtzman*

## A TOWN SQUARE BOOK

**Voyageur Press**

Edited by Margret Aldrich
Designed by Maria Friedrich
Printed in Hong Kong

01    02    03    04    05    5    4    3    2    1

Library of Congress Cataloging-in-Publication Data

Holtzman, Stan, 1942–
     Big rigs : the complete history of the American semi truck / text and photography by
Stan Holtzman.
        p. cm.
     Includes index.
     ISBN 0-89658-495-X
        1. Tractor trailer combinations—United States—History.  I. Title.

     TL230.5.T73 H63 2001
     629.224'0973—dc21                          00-043800

Distributed in Canada by Raincoast Books, 9050 Shaughnessy Street, Vancouver, B.C. V6P 6E5

Published by Voyageur Press, Inc.
123 North Second Street, P.O. Box 338, Stillwater, MN 55082 U.S.A.
651-430-2210, fax 651-430-2211
books@voyageurpress.com
www.voyageurpress.com

*On the frontispiece:* **1971 Peterbilt 352**
*In this 1971 photograph, we see Kenneth Knapp's new Peterbilt Model 352 at Engs Peterbilt. Knapp pulled for Pirkle Refrigerated Lines of Madison, Wisconsin.*

*On the title page:* **1999 International Eagles**
*Several Internationals are lined up for the International Truck Show in Las Vegas, Nevada.*

*Title page inset:* **1947 Autocar advertisement**

*Opposite page:* **Truckers welcome**
*Truckers pull into a favorite watering hole, the Boise Stage Stop in Idaho, for food and fuel. Today's truck stops have become travel centers for both truckers and vacationers alike.*

*Opposite the Contents page:* **1990s Freightliner XL**
*Photographed here is a long-hood XL Model, owned by Wayne and Opal Smith of Chattanooga, Tennessee. This rig runs coast-to-coast hauling refrigerated commodities.*

# Dedication

This book is dedicated to the men and women who do not work for large government agencies and who are not "politically correct" in the eyes of corporate America, because they tend to tell it like it is and are willing to pay the price for being the free-spirited individuals that they are.

# Acknowledgments

I would like to thank the following people, in alphabetical order: Eusebio Ayala, Monterrey, NL, Mexico; Dean Berg of the Harvest Hay Company, Fontana, California; Thomas Boyd, Diamond Bar, California; Gary Bricken, Live Oak, Texas; Joe Cabral of L.A.–Eureka Lines, Montebello, California; Dave Calhoun, Camp Verde, Arizona; "Diesel Dave" Condon, Bellingham, Massachusetts; Kent Gilman, Yorba Linda, California; Hank Hamilton, Chino Hills, California; Gill Hansen of United Van Lines, Snohomish, Washington; Bill Hudgins of *RoadKing* magazine, Nashville, Tennessee; Terry Klenske of Dalton Trucking, Fontana, California; Allan Koenig of Midwest Specialized Transportation, Rochester, Minnesota; Dave Kolman of *Truck Sales & Leasing* magazine, Baltimore, Maryland; Kurtt International Truck Sales and Service, San Jose, Watsonville, and Gilroy, California; Dan Linss of *10-4 Express* magazine, Huntington Beach, California; Bill Martin of Martin Media, Owasso, Oklahoma; Bill Mortimer of the Boerner Truck Center, Huntington Park, California; Joe Mustang, South El Monte, California; Gene Olson of Fort Lauderdale, Florida; Jim Rowe of Roscoe Wagner Livestock Transportation, Twin Falls, Idaho; Sheesley Trucks, Phoenix, Arizona; Cal Smith, Springfield, Missouri; Dick Smith, Victorville, California; Shirley Sponholtz of the American Truck Historical Society, Birmingham, Alabama; RJ Taylor and Ol' Blue® USA, Van Nuys, California; Oklahoma Truck Supply, Tonkawa; Ken Weiland of Weiland Trucking, Sylmar, California; Bill West, Westlake Village, California; Alan Wheeler of Wheeler Freightways, Incorporated, Las Vegas, Nevada; Gerald Williams, Durant, Oklahoma; and Philip Wolff, Albert Lea, Minnesota.

# Contents

# Introduction
## The Fascination of Big Rigs

There is a certain mystique and romance surrounding the people who drive the big rigs, whether they drive locally or long distance. The idea of sitting behind the wheel of a semi with a long expanse of highway stretched out before you holds a feeling of adventure and independence for many, and the trucker often personifies these virtues. Much folklore surrounds the lives of truckers, and Hollywood has done its share to contribute to the legend of this "industry that never sleeps" with movies like *They Drive By Night, White Line Fever,* and *Smokey and the Bandit.*

Whether they own their own truck or drive for a company, truckers are a special breed of individual. Because of the amount of self-reliance truckers must possess, other people's attitudes about them can be both envious and admiring. However, as they go about their business without much notice or fanfare, the contributions of these generally honest and hardworking people are often overlooked.

Truckers come in all shapes, colors, sizes, and genders, yet they have one thing in common: the love of freedom. Different than the employee who works all day on his or her computer in a small office, truckers cannot work in a structured corporate environment. While truckers do not have the luxury of regular 9 A.M. to 5 P.M. hours, three to four weeks per year of paid vacation, a 401(k) plan, or medical insurance, they have chosen their place in life and have no regrets, as their "office" is the open road.

The people who drive trucks can rightly be called the pulse of America, because they are the individuals who haul food, lumber, and other necessities from coast to coast. But like many of us, truckers might be driving an older Chevy or Toyota when not behind the wheel of a big rig. They may also be parents, working hard to raise their children well. Truckers have many of the same trials, tribulations, and celebrations that we do, and, like the rest of us, they are a reflection of our society and a part of what keeps the country moving.

This book is a tribute to truckers and the rigs they drive. While every make and model could not be represented in these pages, all of the major American truck manufacturers, and many of the minor ones, appear here. I hope that in this book you are able to find a rig that you've had the pleasure to drive, or one that you have simply admired as it rolled down the highway.

*Top:* **1977 Smokey and the Bandit promotional poster**

*Bottom:* **1951 Peterbilt ad**

*Opposite page:* **1964 Kenworth**
*Truckers could still order the older-style Kenworth cab with its smaller windshield area as late as 1964. Robert Phair ran this dark metallic green KW from Washington to California until the 1980s.*

# CHAPTER 1

# Autocar

## *Setting the Standard*

*Above:* **1946 Autocar advertisement**

*Left:* **1970s Autocar**
*A heavy-duty Autocar wrecker is seen here, parked and ready for any emergency. Don's Makiki Service of Honolulu, Hawaii, owned this rig, photographed in 1975.*

The Autocar Company had a long history building trucks, as it got its start in 1897 by brothers Louis and John Clarke in Pittsburgh, Pennsylvania. Originally dubbed the Pittsburgh Motor Vehicle Company, it took the name Autocar in 1899 and began production in Ardmore, Pennsylvania, in 1900.

As a pioneer in automotive expertise, Autocar was the first to make a universal shaft-driven vehicle and can also be credited with being the first automaker to use porcelain-insulated spark plugs. Always an innovator, Autocar was also ahead of its time in the 1920s, when it was one of the first in the industry to use electricity as an alternate source of power for its trucks.

In 1908, "A-Car" (as Autocar was commonly refered to) was one of the first manufacturers to come out with a cab-over-engine (COE) model. The cab-over design, which allowed the driver to sit above the truck's engine, became popular in the 1920s and remained so well into the 1980s. The design, which gave the driver better visibility and a tighter turning radius, was especially helpful in congested cities where turning could be a problem. Class 8 trucks, which are trucks that weigh over 33,000 pounds (14,982 kg) and are what we know as "big rigs" today, were popular as cab-overs from the 1940s through the 1980s in order to combat strict length laws, as well as to allow more payload space.

In the 1930s, Autocar's newly designed cab-over, the U Model, hit the highways. The U Model followed the more streamlined, art deco style of the time, had a set-back front axle, and featured "suicide" doors, which had hinges on the back and opened from the front.

Like much of its competition, Autocar became a popular truck for fire departments on both coasts because of its dependability and sturdy construction. Although Autocar built some three-axle fire trucks, most were made as two-axle models.

With the onset of World War II, Autocar geared up its production for the military by making armor-plated vehicles in the form of half-tracks (armored vehicles that had tracks like an army tank on its rear axles, and regular truck tires on its front axle). During the early 1940s, Autocar was allowed to make 3,000 vehicles for civilian use, but it was after the war that Autocar's sales really started to take off, and their nameplate became a common sight across the United States. In the East, the Autocar was especially popular as a heavy-equipment hauler, while out West the Autocar was the choice of those in the professions of hauling freight, logs, livestock, and petroleum.

With its two-piece flat windshield, Autocar was available either as a low-mount or high-mount conventional, which is a truck that has its hood and engine in front of the cab. While the low-mount cab allowed easier entry for the driver, the high-mount provided better visibility of the road that lay ahead.

Around 1950, the Autocar cab was completely redesigned with a two-piece, slightly curved windshield. So popular was this cab, that other companies, such as the White Motor Company of Cleveland, Ohio; the Diamond T Motor Company of Chicago, Illinois; Western Star Trucks of Kelowna, British Columbia, Canada; and Dina Diesel Nacional of Monterrey, N.L., Mexico, began making a similar cab for some of their models of trucks.

In 1953, the White Motor Company took over Autocar, but unlike the Sterling Motors Corporation of Milwaukee, Wisconsin, another of White's acquisitions, the Autocar would not be phased out of production. The basic Autocar cab of the 1950s was altered very little in overall appearance after the change in ownership, but by the late 1980s, it had taken on the look of its White-GMC sister rigs, as a true member of the White family of trucks. Autocar would eventually become a part of the Volvo-White Truck Corporation in Greensboro, North Carolina, after Volvo acquired White.

As part of Volvo Trucks, Autocars were highly regarded by the construction and refuse industries throughout the 1980s and 1990s. However, in July 2000, Volvo announced that production of all Autocar models would end. The over-one-hundred-year-old name in trucking was to be replaced by the new Volvo VHD, an on- and off-highway truck designed for severe-duty vocational applications. Shown to be 50 percent more reliable than its leading competitors in a durability test, the VHD proved to be a truck that the time-honored Autocar could not beat.

**1940s Autocar tanker**

*C&C Transportation of Paramount, California, ran this Autocar well into the 1980s, hauling hot liquid asphalt.*

**1943 Autocar advertisement**

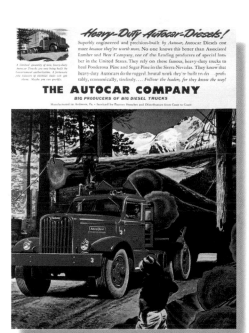

**1947 Autocar advertisement**

**1941 Autocar**

*Virgil Pierce drove this Autocar for LaSalle Trucking. Colors were two-tone orange with black fenders. Based in San Diego, California, LaSalle is a longtime LTL (less-than-truckload) freight line.*

**1947 Autocar advertisement**

**1940s Autocar advertisement**

**1940s Autocar**
*An Autocar from Gary, Indiana, is seen here with an integral sleeper at Mike & Vic's Truck Stop in 1965.*

**1956 Autocar advertisement**

**1950s Autocar**
*Autocars are known for their ruggedness—Coastal Equipment used this A-Car in the oil fields near Bakersfield, California. You won't find any fiberglass or lightweight aluminum on this tough truck!*

**1959 Autocar DC 10264**
*Autocars are always a favorite at truck shows across the country. This A-Car, owned by Karl B. Hertz of Claremont, California, proudly sits on display at a show in Riverside, California.*

**1950s Autocar livestock rig**
*In this 1957 photograph, one of Washum Brothers' Autocar cattle trucks is parked at the Los Angeles Union Stockyards in Vernon, California, after unloading some Arizona livestock. Washum is still in business, operating under the name of L.A. Yuma Freight Lines, no longer hauling livestock but hauling LTL freight.*

**1960s Autocar**
*The Southern Screw Company of Statesville, North Carolina, ran this dark green 1960s integral-sleeper Autocar to the West Coast every week. It pulled a 40-foot (12.2-m) trailer produced by the Fruehauf Trailer Company.*

**1968 Autocar A Model brochure**

**1960s Autocar**
*This Autocar is set up as a cement-mixer in Puerto Rico. Notice how far the front bumper is from the rest of the cab; it is made of heavy gauge steel to handle any off-road problem.*

**1965 Autocar**
*Cliff Morris of Pandora, Ohio, sits in his new Autocar at a Cummins Diesel garage in Perrysburg, Ohio. The sleeper appears to be from a Kenworth, and the colors of this rig are two-tone turquoise.*

**1970s Autocar**
*In this 1986 photograph, Angel Soto's Autocar is running down a road near San Juan, Puerto Rico. This rig has heavy steel front fenders.*

**1980s Autocar**
*Pate Construction Company of North Providence, Rhode Island, ran this Autocar, photographed here in 1988. Autocars have always been a popular truck in the construction industry.*

**1976 Autocar brochure**

**1980s Autocar AT64**
*Belger Cartage, in business since 1919, ran this black beauty coast-to-coast. The photo shown here was taken in Las Vegas, Nevada.*

*Left:* **1988 Autocar**
*Autocars of this era were geared for construction and refuse hauling. Note the White-GMC nameplate that appears on this truck's front grille.*

**1980s Autocar AT64**
*This metallic blue Autocar, circa 1984, hauled liquid commodities cross-country for Erickson Transport of Springfield, Missouri.*

**VOLVO AUTOCAR TRUCKS**
*Specifications and Equipment*

**VOLVO**

**1997 Volvo Autocar brochure**

# Brockway

## The Husky Heavyweight

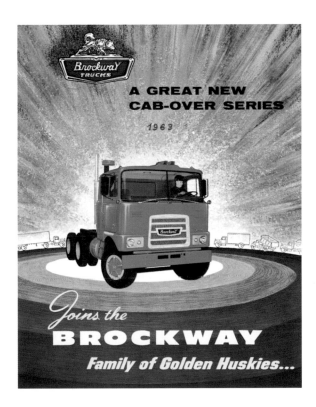

*Above:* **1963 Brockway advertisement**

*Left:* **1950s Brockway**
*In this 1965 photo, a 1950s workhorse loaded with steel is pulling for the Glenn Cartage Company of Youngstown, Ohio.*

William N. Brockway founded the Brockway Carriage Factory in Homer, New York, in 1851. His son, George A. Brockway, took over the reins in 1889, and by 1912, the Brockway Motor Truck Company had been formed and a new location in Cortland, New York, became the base of all operations.

In 1914, conventional trucks with up to 2,300 pounds (1,044 kg) of weight capacity and four-cylinder gasoline engines from the Continental Motors Corporation of Muskegon, Michigan, were being produced by Brockway. In 1925, the company offered both four- and six-cylinder engines in its line-up of trucks but, by 1928, had phased out the four-cylinder entirely and only offered a six-cylinder Continental engine.

During World War I, Brockway produced many trucks for the military, including 587 Class B "Liberty" trucks between 1917 and 1918. By the close of the 1920s, Brockway was one of the largest independent producers of motor trucks in the United States for both military and civilian use, with 5,500 rigs being made annually. The acquisition of the Indiana Truck Company of Marion, Indiana, in 1928 also enhanced production figures, but when the Great Depression hit in the early 1930s, Brockway sold off Indiana Truck to the White Motor Corporation in order to remain afloat and focused on making Brockway trucks.

From 1933 to 1937, in addition to producing gasoline-powered trucks, Brockway made electric-powered trucks that could haul from 1- to 7-ton (0.9- to 6.4-t) loads. By 1940, Brockway was making tractors to pull semi trailers that were capable of moving 10-ton (9.1-t) loads, still using the reliable Continental gasoline engines of that era. Continental was the major supplier of engines for Brockway trucks until the 1960s, when diesel engines from companies such as the Cummins Engine Company of Columbus, Indiana; the Detroit Diesel Engine Division of General Motors of Detroit, Michigan; and the Caterpillar Engine Company of Peoria, Illinois, phased out the older gasoline engines.

With the onset of World War II, Brockway was called upon to assist in the war effort. The company met the challenge by making a 6-ton (5.5-t) 6x6 truck that was used to transport the rubber pontoons and steel treadways needed to make military combat bridges. Later, that same truck was further adapted as a load carrier, a crane carrier, and as an airfield crash unit.

It was after the war that Brockway introduced its popular 260 Series, which offered both trucks and tractors, complete with integral sleepers for long-haul use. These Brockways were able to pull loads from 20,000 to 65,000 pounds (9,080–29,510 kg), and their wood and steel cab construction made them long-lasting trucks.

On October 1, 1956, Brockway became part of Mack Trucks, Incorporated of Allentown, Pennsylvania, and in 1958, Brockway's famous Husky hood ornament made its debut and took its place alongside the Mack Bulldog which had come out in the 1940s. Like the Bulldog that proudly graced the hood of every Mack, the chrome Husky rode on the front of every Brockway, pointing the rig down the highway. In 1962, the Husky was gold-plated to commemorate Brockway's golden anniversary.

Using an F Model Mack, Brockway constructed their own line of cab-overs, the 400 Series, in 1963. The only visible difference between Mack's F Model and Brockway's entry in the cab-over market was in the trucks' grille designs.

In 1971, Brockway unleashed the "Huskiteer," a low-entry cab-over made for inner-city use where heavy traffic and tight turning presented problems. Although the Huskiteer and Brockway's other cab-overs were capable trucks, they were not very popular with truckers because they so closely resembled the F Model Mack, and Mack had the advantage of having more dealers across the country and was marketed more aggressively.

In April 1977, after an unauthorized strike by the local union, Brockway's production ground to a halt, and on June 8, 1977, their last truck, serial number 91863, rolled out of the factory and into trucking history.

**1970s Brockway**

*In this 1988 photograph, we see a Brockway that was traded in on a new Kenworth at a Kenworth dealers facility in New England.*

**1960s Brockway**

*A Brockway cab-over, circa 1963, is seen here. It looks a lot like the F Model Mack of the 1960s, except that the front grille is different in design.*

**1970s Brockway**

*This Brockway is seen running down a Connecticut highway in 1988. Brockways were a popular truck in the New England area in the 1960s through the 1980s.*

**1970s Brockway**

*While surviving Brockways can still be seen in the eastern United States from time to time, many trucks like this ones found a new home in Puerto Rico, and remained in use through the 1980s and into the 1990s.*

# Chevrolet

## *A Key Player*

*Above:* **1954 Chevrolet advertisement**

*Left:* **1960s Chevrolet**
*It took plenty of guts to run this little Chevy cross-country—especially without a sleeper! This photograph was taken in Tucson, Arizona, in 1967.*

ost people associate the name Chevrolet with both a popular make of automobile and a builder of smaller trucks for the General Motors Corporation of Detroit, Michigan.

The Chevrolet Division of General Motors actually got into making small pickup and delivery trucks as early as 1918, but ultimately had less of an impact on trucking than did their rival, the Ford Motor Company, also of Detroit.

In the 1920s and early 1930s, Chevy offered various models of their truck for both farm and city use, but it wasn't until the mid-1930s that Chevrolet went after the bigger truck market.

The 1930s brought new innovations to Chevy trucks. By 1936, Chevrolet had redesigned their line-up to conform with the popular streamlined look by lowering the roof of their cabs. Hydraulic brakes also became a standard item. Short wheelbase 1½-ton (1.4-t) models were being converted into tractors for pulling 16- to 24-foot (4.9- to 7.3-m) trailers, and by the end of the decade, cab-overs were being offered by Chevrolet.

Chevrolet did its part in the war effort of the early 1940s by providing the armed forces with a variety of light and armored vehicles. After World War II, the basic Chevy design of trucks looked much like their straightforward 1941–1942 models, with very few noticeable physical changes. The year 1947, however, brought a dramatic change to the style of the Chevrolet truck, and sales began to rise. The '47 Chevy had newly designed cab doors, a two-piece windshield, headlights that were built into the front fenders, and horizontal bars adorning the grille.

Chevy was still primarily making smaller trucks, but in 1952, produced a model that featured a 90-hp, four-cylinder, two-stroke engine from the Detroit Diesel Engine Division of General Motors. However, the model found little success, due to the fact that it was newly developed and hadn't had time enough to be proven a workhorse. Detroit Desiel engines were not as popular as gasoline engines were in these smaller trucks. However, Detroit Diesels became very desirable engines and continue to be offered in big rigs today.

In 1955, Chevy came out with another newly designed cab, which featured a wraparound windshield, like those on the cars produced by Chevrolet, and a 12-volt electrical system. The following year, V-8 engines in Chevy trucks began gaining popularity, and tubeless tires started to become standard equipment. In 1957, air-over-hydraulic brakes came into being, and in 1958, a full air-brake system was in place.

The next decade had Chevrolet looking farther into the future. Around 1965, Chevy, along with Ford, started experimenting with gas turbine-powered engines, and the aerodynamics of both the Ford and Chevy models of this era provided a glimpse into what trucking would look like in the forthcoming millennium. Square lines gave way to smoother, more rounded styling, providing less wind resistance and better fuel mileage.

By 1970, Chevrolet was widely known as a credible builder of Class 8 diesel trucks, with the advent of the famous Titan cab-over. Engines for the Titan were available as a V-6, V-8, or a V-12 from Detroit Diesel. The Titan was equipped with power steering, air suspension, and either a 10- or 13-speed transmission. The cab-over also offered either a day cab (non-sleeper cab) or a sleeper cab for the long-distance trucker. In 1977, Chevy introduced the Bison, a new conventional model. The Bison boasted engines with up to 430 hp, which were offered by Detroit Diesel, as well as Cummins.

Although both were powerful machines, the Titan and the Bison were short-lived because they looked just like their counterparts in the GMC line of Class 8 trucks, but were not as widely accepted. The Chevrolet Titan cab-over looked much like GMC's Astro 95, which came out in 1968, and the Bison closely resembled its cousin, the GMC General, which came out in the early 1970s. Because the manufacturing of these Chevys that differed from their GMC duplicates in nameplate alone was not cost-effective, Chevrolet stopped their production in the late 1970s. While today Chevy no longer builds the larger Class 8 rigs, the company remains quite successful with its smaller line of trucks.

**1960s Chevrolet**
*This Chevy cab-over ran interstate, promoting Chevrolet cars and trucks. It is shown here in Arizona in 1968.*

**1960 Chevrolet advertisement**

**1966 Chevrolet advertisement**

**1970s Chevrolet Bison**
*This rare Bison, owned by United Rock Products of Irwindale, California, is set up as a water truck. The Bison lasted for only a few short years, but its "twin," the GMC General, enjoyed success on both coasts of the country.*

**YOUR MONEY'S WORTH. MILE AFTER MILE AFTER MILE.**

1975 Chevrolet Titan 90 brochure

# Diamond T /Reo

## A Chicago-Born Success

***Above: 1960s Diamond T***
*Amway Home Products of Ada, Michigan, ran this Diamond T cab-over cross-country, carrying their products to various warehouses. This photograph was taken at the Triple T Truck Stop in Tucson, Arizona, in 1967.*

***Left: 1940s and 1950s Diamond Ts***
*Several different models of Diamond T trucks are shown at an antique truck show in Portland, Oregon, which was put on by the American Truck Historical Society.*

aming a company after a brand of shoes is a strange way to start a business, but that's exactly what Charles A. Tilt did when, in 1905, he built his first car, and the Diamond T Motor Company of Chicago, Illinois, made its debut. Tilt's father was a shoemaker, whose imprint was a green diamond outlined in gold, standing for quality, with a "T" in the center, standing for Tilt. It was only natural for young Charles to follow in his dad's footsteps with a similar logo for his new vehicles. Automobile production took place until around 1911, when one of Tilt's customers wanted a truck to be built—the rest, as they say, is history.

By 1915, Diamond T was starting to grow, with factory branches and dealers popping up all over the country. The company began taking root in some Latin American and European countries as well.

With the onset of World War I, the government appointed Diamond T to make 1,500 3- to 5-ton (2.7- to 4.5-t) "Liberty" trucks in a time-span of only eighteen months, and the challenge was met.

In the 1920s, Diamond T was on a roll, with more orders coming in from both government and civilian patrons. Prices for the various models of Diamond Ts ranged from around $2,000 to over $5,600—a lot of money, in those days, for a truck.

Buyers got their money's worth, however, with the quality-conscious and innovative trucks. Pneumatic tires started to appear on the Diamond T as early as 1921, and left-hand steering came out that same year.

Diamond T was not timid in their use of chrome, and in the late 1920s, chrome could be found on such items as headlights, moldings, parking lights, and runningboards—all of which made the competition look ordinary.

The heavy use of chrome continued into the 1930s and could be seen in larger hubcaps and in the grille areas of the smaller pickup trucks that were produced alongside Diamond T's panel trucks. An integral sleeper cab was offered this decade as well, to the delight of truckers running long distances.

The 1940s brought several successes and changes to the company. During World War II, Diamond T produced over 50,000 vehicles of various sizes for the military. In 1946, C. A. Tilt retired after forty-one years

with the company, but the popularity of Diamond T continued to increase. Sales started to climb in 1947, and Diamond T decided to phase out the building of smaller trucks in order to concentrate on making the larger Class 8 rigs.

In 1951, Diamond T received another face-lift, with its newly designed cab, made by the Chicago Manufacturing Company. It had a semi-wraparound one-piece windshield, a more rounded roof line, and a front grille with horizontal bars. So popular was this cab that other truck makers, such as the International Harvester Company of Chicago, Illinois; the Hendrickson Manufacturing Company of Lyons, Illinois; the American Coleman Company of Littleton, Colorado; the Oshkosh Truck Corporation of Oshkosh, Wisconsin; and the FWD Corporation of Clintonville, Wisconsin, decided to use the design when producing their own trucks.

In the early 1950s, a new cab-over called the 923C was a big hit with truckers. The rig had a large two-piece panoramic windshield and remained in production until 1961. Also built in the 1950s were Models 950 and 951, which were Diamond T's largest trucks. These conventional models sat as high as many cab-overs and had much larger radiators to facilitate the bigger diesel engines that were replacing gasoline-powered motors.

It was in the late 1950s that both Diamond T and the Reo Motor Car Company of Lansing, Michigan, were bought by the White Motor Company, which ultimately resulted in a new truck called the Diamond Reo. Thus, no history on Diamond T would be complete unless we backtrack and delve into the Reo Motor Car Company.

The name Reo was formed from the initials of Ransom E. Olds of Oldsmobile fame, when he founded the company in 1904. Like many truck makers, Reo began building automobiles first, but by 1913, Reo was making its famous Speedwagon, a best-selling truck for ten years. Various models of the Speedwagon were produced from the 1920s well into the 1930s. Reo could also boast of being the first truck maker, from 1932 to 1934, to offer a straight-8 engine—and you thought that Packard or Pontiac was famous for this engine!

Reo did its share for the war effort in the 1940s, by

making everything from buses to 6x6 trucks and tractors with Continental gas-powered six-cylinder engines.

After the war, the Reo took on a look that resembled the K Model Internationals and sported a new engine called the Gold Comet with an OHV six-cylinder motor. In 1956, Reo began offering diesel engines in their larger models.

It was in 1957 that Reo, followed by Diamond T in 1958, became part of the White Motor Company. Both Diamond T and Reo shared the same Lansing location for building trucks, but each retained a separate division. This would soon end, however. The last truck to bear the Diamond T name was made toward the end of 1966; in 1967, the two divisions consolidated completely and became Diamond Reo.

All seemed to be going well for Diamond Reo, but financial problems eventually led to bankruptcy in 1975. Two years later, Diamond Reo was bought by Osterlund, Incorporated of Harrisburg, Pennsylvania, who produced Diamond Reos into the 1980s. In 1993, Osterlund sold the company, and the New Diamond T Company was formed in Harrisburg, with most of its new trucks being made for export.

**1950s Diamond T 923 C**
*An early-1950s cab-over is getting its Keystone livestock trailer washed out at the Los Angeles Union Stockyards in this 1956 photo.*

**1938 Diamond T advertisement**

**1950s Reo**
*A rare Reo cab-over, circa 1956. This rig was built before Diamond T and Reo merged to become Diamond Reo.*

**1950s Diamond T 920 brochure**

**1950s Diamond T**
*Ed Rodela of Rosemead, California, is seen here atop his trailer loading steel structures. The Diamond T cab of the 1950s was also used by International trucks.*

**1960s Diamond T**
*This 1965 photograph shows a new Diamond T pulling a 40-foot (12.2-m) Fruehauf furniture trailer for the Baker Furniture Company of Grand Rapids, Michigan. The photo was taken in Perrysburg, Ohio.*

**1960s Diamond T**

*F & B Truck Line of Salt Lake City, Utah, ran this red Diamond T. Notice that the cab resembles that of the Autocar. F & B ran in the West, hauling flatbed freight.*

**The diamond is for quality!**
Diamond T ad, 1962

**1960s Diamond T**
*This Diamond T, circa 1965, was based in Texas and sported a very small sleeper behind its cab. Hey, what happened to that right exhaust stack?*

**1960s Diamond T**

*This photograph, taken in 1969 at Jerrell's Truck Plaza in Doswell, Virginia, features a cab-over with a sleeper, pulling for Pilot Freight Carriers of Winston-Salem, North Carolina.*

**1960s Diamond T**
*Check out those diamond-plated steel front fenders on this Puerto Rican Diamond T—and how about the area protecting the headlights!*

**1970s Diamond T**
*In this photograph taken near Fresno, California, in 1975, we see a Diamond T truck and trailer set up to haul petroleum.*

**1970s Diamond Reo Raider brochure**

C H A P T E R    5

# Dodge

## *Defining Dependability*

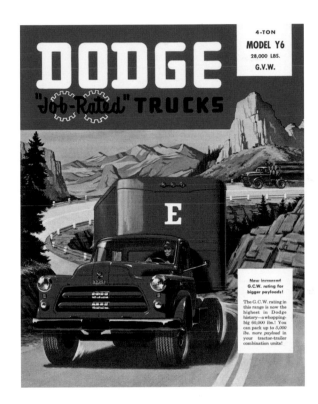

*Above:* **1950s Dodge Y6 brochure**

*Left:* **1973 Dodge Bighorn**
*A rare Dodge Bighorn tractor is shown here at a park in Glendale, California. The Bighorn was built in the early 1970s, and only about fifty are known to exist today.*

When brothers Horace and John Dodge started building bicycles in the Detroit area in the late 1800s, they probably had no idea that their venture would lead to a successful truck-manufacturing business and an eventual consolidation with one of the biggest automotive corporations in the country. But this is precisely what happened when Walter P. Chrysler, founder of the Chrysler Corporation of Detroit, Michigan, took over Dodge in 1928, eight years after the deaths of both Dodge brothers. This chapter will focus on the Class 8 rigs produced by this giant in trucks.

Under the Chrysler Corporation, the Dodge Division prospered, while other truck makers became casualties of the Great Depression. The early 1930s were known as the Glamour Era in the company's history, as Dodge trucks from that period reflected the art deco look, though their trucks were small in size. This decade also saw the first diesel engines being used in Dodge trucks, appearing in 1939.

As World War II loomed, Dodge geared up for what was to be an important role for this truck maker in the 1940s. During the war, Dodge built all sorts of trucks for the military, from ½-ton (0.5-t) models up to 6x6 units, and out of this came the famous Power Wagon, still in demand today. The Power Wagon was the size of a pickup truck and was designed for both off- and on-highway use. The entire front end, including the cab, fenders, and hood, were all steel and had a functional, military style. These characteristics contributed to the truck's popularity with civilians as an off-road sports vehicle.

It was also in the 1940s that Dodge made the "Job Rated" trucks that would set the stage for the larger Class 8 rigs of the 1960s. These reliable trucks could be seen in use in the construction and farming industries, as well as by utility companies.

Dodge became a serious contender in the Class 8 truck-making field in the '60s, and the diesel engine became the power of choice in Dodge trucks. With the dawning of this decade, Dodge developed a new line of larger trucks, called the C Series. These trucks featured a short cab with fenders that could swing out so servicing the engine would be more mechanic-friendly. This series was to replace the traditional forward-conventional models. The Dodge C cab conventional became popular as the decade continued, especially among truckers who transported automobiles, as well as for certain applications in the construction industry. The C cab could be ordered either as a two-axle or as a three-axle, depending on the weight of the load to be carried.

In 1964, Dodge came out with the L Series—an impressive-looking cab-over that offered a sleeper cab as an option. The L Series shared the same status as any rig from Pacific Car and Foundry (PACCAR) of Kirkland, Washington, or the White Motor Company's White-Freightliner Division, both in its size and its place in the cab-over market. The model was popular with freight lines as well as with the moving and storage industries.

As the 1970s approached, Dodge came out with their largest conventional truck, the Bighorn, but its run was short-lived. Of the less than three hundred Dodge Bighorns that were made from 1972 to 1975, there are only about fifty that are known to exist today, making them a highly collectible truck.

Dodge eventually decided to stop building their larger Class 8 trucks, although the L Series had been a proven success, and in 1975, all production of both their cab-overs and conventional models came to a halt.

Currently, Dodge has returned to what it knows best: making smaller trucks. The company continues to find success, and its Ram pickup truck is one of Dodge's most popular vehicles to date.

**1960s Dodge**
*Taken near Toledo, Ohio, in 1965, this photograph features what appears to be an early-1960s model two-axle Dodge pulling a single axle trailer for the Square Deal Cartage Company.*

**1950s Dodge advertisement**

**1960s Dodge**
*Jaime Rodarte of Montebello, California, ran this rare 1960s Dodge transfer-dump in the Los Angeles area well into the 1990s.*

**1964 Dodge L**

*Thurlow Spur and "The Spurlows," brought the sounds of music to many a local high school in the 1960s thanks to this L Model Dodge. With the sponsorship of the Chrysler Corporation, this blue and white cab-over could be seen at high schools across the nation.*

**1970 Dodge L**
*A new L Model Dodge with a sleeper cab is seen here at an Anaheim, California, truck show. From the looks of its colors, this truck might have belonged to Whiting Brothers of Holbrook, Arizona, to deliver fuel to the many gas stations that they once owned.*

**A big rarin'-to-go engine . . . high-powered for heavy hauling.**
Dodge brochure, 1950s

**DODGE TRUCKS**
Heavy-Duty Tilt Cab Diesel Models

**1972 Dodge brochure**

# Federal

## *Never an Experiment*

*Above:* **1940 Federal advertisement**

*Left:* **1940s Federal**
*There is no room for wimpy fiberglass or aluminum on this mighty Federal tow truck, which was converted to civilian use after World War II. The beast was built to take a world of punishment, as this 1966 photo depicts.*

Many books on trucking fail to mention the Federal Motor Truck Company of Detroit, Michigan, but there was a time when Federal was a serious competitor in the field of truck manufacturing.

In February 1910, Martin L. Pulcher of Detroit started the Bailey Motor Truck Company, renamed the Federal Motor Truck Company later that year, with $50,000 and served as both President and General Manager. The company's first truck was called the Federal and was a factory-assembled truck throughout its history. Federals were traditionally built as conventionals, although a cab-over was later introduced in 1937.

In the 1920s, Federal conventional trucks came in a variety of sizes, from 1½-ton (1.4-t) models up to 5-ton (4.5-t) rigs with six-cylinder Continental engines providing their power.

By the late '20s, pneumatic tires started appearing on the larger Federal models, and the company boasted one of the first sleeper cabs on its larger tractors. Front wheel brakes were also starting to be seen, with Federal having vacuum-operated hydraulic braking systems.

Federal was making trucks that ranged in size from 1 to 8 tons (0.9 to 7.3 t) by the 1930s, which were powered by engines from Continental, the Hercules Motors Corporation of Canton, Ohio, or the Waukesha Motor Company of Waukesha, Wisconsin. In these pre-war years, Federal offered sleeper cabs on their larger models, which used 115-hp Waukesha and 138-hp Continental gasoline engines.

In 1934, styling changes brought a more streamlined look to the rig, with the advent of the one-piece, slightly slanted, visorless windshield. By 1935, Federal trucks had gotten another face-lift, with the addition of fender skirts to some of their models and more chrome to all, making the Federal as attractive as most of the cars with which it shared the road.

So successful was the Detroit-based company, that a Canadian factory in Windsor, Ontario, was built in the 1930s in order to handle increasing business. As the decade came to a close, eighteen different models were offered, ranging in price from $645 to $5,345, with the 6-ton (5.4-t) Federal being the most popular model. By 1939, Federal had made its one-hundred-thousandth truck.

During World War II Federal made large 6x6 7½-ton (6.8-t) wreckers that became quite popular as heavy-duty tow trucks for civilian use after the war. It was during the war years that Federal made its biggest truck yet, a 20-ton (18.1-t) 6x4 tractor that was used for moving heavy military equipment. This truck had a 130-hp Cummins six-cylinder diesel engine.

In 1951, a newly designed Styliner was made, bringing with it a brand new look. It had a one-piece, slightly curved windshield and a front grille that featured thick, chromed vertical bars running from the front bumper up to the hood opening. The Styliner's hood opened much like the hoods of automobiles from that era; a one-piece bonnet was raised up after unlatching it from the front. The new look did not prove to be a success, however, and sales started to decline.

The company continued to make some specialty vehicles for the U.S. Air Force and some snow-plow rigs. In 1954, Federal also built an unusual vehicle that deviated from their philosophy of going along with what the competition was doing and not experimenting with proven success; it was called the "Octo-Quad," which used the front of a large bus as its cab.

These ventures were not enough to keep Federal in business, however, and sadly production came to a halt for all intents and purposes in March 1959. The total number of trucks made by Federal was estimated to be about 160,000 units.

*Left:* 1950s Federal 4551 spec sheet

*Right:* 1950s Federal 6501 spec sheet

**1940s Federal**

*This Federal was used locally to pick up and deliver LTL freight for Milne Truck Lines in and around the St. George area of Utah. This photograph was taken in 1965.*

**1950s Federal**

*Photographed at a Pure Oil truck stop in Perrysburg, Ohio, in 1965, this Federal, known as the "Leprechaun," pulled many a load of steel in and around Detroit, Pittsburgh, and Toledo.*

# CHAPTER 7

# Ford

## *Proven Popularity*

**Above: 1960s Ford H**
*Although this "Two-Story Falcon," circa 1965, had a sleeper, it afforded little room in which to move around. This photograph was taken at Jerrell's Truck Plaza in Doswell, Virginia, in 1967.*

**Left: 1990s Ford AeroMax**
*Truck shows always seem to bring out the very best in equipment, as can be seen at this Las Vegas, Nevada, event. Parked together are two impressive AeroMax tractors.*

Most of us know about the early beginnings of Henry Ford, his "Tin Lizzie," and the many models of both cars and smaller trucks that the corporate giant produced over the past century. This chapter specifically explores the Ford Motor Company of Detroit, Michigan, as a viable competitor in the field of Class 8 trucks.

The evolution of Ford's larger trucks began after World War II, with the birth of the F Series of Ford trucks. These trucks, which debuted in 1948, were offered from the F1 to the larger F8 Models, with weights ranging from 2½-ton (2.3-t) trucks to the larger 3-ton (2.7-t) rigs. The Ford trucks of the F Series were powered by Lincoln V-8 gasoline engines and featured standard air brakes on the bigger models.

Around 1956, the famous C Model cab-over was introduced, with its two-piece wraparound windshield. This truck was quite popular when set up as a straight truck, or "bobtail," but eventually grew into a well-respected three-axle tractor with an optional small sleeper cab. Three axles are common for Class 8 tractors, because this allows one to steer and two to support the weight of the load. The C Model was a favorite with the nation's freight lines for use in local pick up and delivery of less-than-truckload, or "LTL," freight, which entails the consolidation of products from several different companies in order to fill up space in the trailer. With its sleeper cab, the C Model found its way into the hearts of long-distance movers hauling furniture as well. Although this Ford was a popular truck, it was finally phased out in the 1990s, after its sales had peaked and the competition began making lighter and more streamlined trucks.

Engines evolved quickly in Ford trucks. By 1959, the company offered diesel engines as an option for their larger trucks, and by 1960, had tested a gas turbine engine. In 1963, Ford dumped a 600-hp engine into an experimental, streamlined cab-over. By the mid-1960s engines in their largest models were provided by Detroit Diesel, Cummins, and Caterpillar.

In 1961, Ford proved that it was serious about capturing the Class 8 truck market with the introduction of the H Model cab-over, or "Two-Story Falcon." The H Model offered the option of a small factory integral sleeper and was a common sight on the nation's Interstates during the 1960s. The conventional NTD Model was soon to follow. Like the H Model, the NTD could facilitate a sleeper, and it served as a powerful example of Ford's Class 8 rigs.

In 1966, the Ford H Model gave way to a newer cab-over, the W Model. Like the H Model and the NTD, it was available as either a day cab or as a sleeper-equipped rig, but the W Model did not live up to the aesthetics of its predecessors. This truck had a rather square look to it, a two-piece flat windshield, and large letters spelling "F-O-R-D" just below the windshield wipers. Even with some added chrome, the W Model's appearance left much to be desired.

Ford built an entirely new Class 8 truck factory in Louisville, Kentucky, in 1969, due to an increase in consumer demand. This plant produced the larger Ford trucks up until the last big rig was built by Ford toward the end of the twentieth century.

In 1970, Ford's conventional L line was being made in Louisville. These trucks featured diesel engines, which were cheaper to operate than gasoline engines, and fiberglass front-ends that could be tilted forward to provide easy access to them. The larger Louisville Fords had an impressive gross vehicle weight (GVW) of 80,000 pounds (36,320 kg). With the help of the L Series, Ford continued to grow in popularity and, in 1974, ranked number three in Class 8 truck sales, just behind International and Mack.

By 1978, the W Model cab-over was retired and replaced by the CL Model. As with previous cab-overs made by Ford, this truck offered a sleeper cab as an option. The CL Model was well-received, as its rounded cab that somewhat resembled Mack's MH Model reflected the style of the times. When a fair amount of chrome was added, this rig could hold its own with any of PACCAR's good-looking trucks from the Kenworth Truck Company of Seattle, Washington, or the Peterbilt Motors Corporation of Denton, Texas.

The CL Ford was manufactured until 1991, when Ford decided to phase out production of its line of cab-over models. The Ford conventional L Series, however, was going strong in sales. With a newly redesigned, more aerodynamic front end, this truck was popular for both fleets and individual truckers alike.

Ford came out with its final Class 8 big rig, the

AeroMax, in 1988. The Louisville-produced AeroMax was a more aerodynamic, advanced design of Ford's famous L Model. With its angled corners and bumpers, flush headlight area, tapered hood, and curved one-piece windshield, the AeroMax experienced less wind resistance, providing the driver with better fuel mileage. So successful was the AeroMax, they are still a common sight on today's highways.

Ford's final year making Class 8 trucks was 1998, as Freightliner then took over Ford's Class 8 operations and reintroduced the name Sterling, which had last been seen on a big rig in 1953. The new Sterlings still closely resemble the Fords that came before them, but they will slowly take on their own identity and no longer look like an AeroMax with an "S" in the middle of its grille.

**1964 Ford H**
*The H Model Ford was often referred to as the "Two-Story Falcon" by truckers. This cab-over, which was painted in two-tone blue, hauled Ford parts in the Toledo-Detroit area in the 1960s.*

**1960s Ford W**
*A Ford W Model with a sleeper cab is parked at the Triple T Truck Stop in Tucson, Arizona, in this photograph from 1967. The unit ran cross-country, hauling U-Haul parts to its many distributors.*

**1947 Ford advertisement illustration**

**1947 Ford advertisement illustration**

**1960s Ford Louisville**
*This late-1960s Ford was photographed pulling a load of cattle in Puerto Rico in 1986.*

*Left:* **1960 Ford advertisement**

**1970s Ford W**
*In this 1975 photograph, we see a W Model Ford traveling a freeway near downtown Honolulu to make a delivery to a construction site.*

**1970s Ford Louisville 9000**

*A Louisville 9000 is seen here pulling an oversize load for Ace Transportation of Oklahoma City, Oklahoma. This photo was taken at The Wheel Inn in Cabazon, California.*

**1980s Ford Louisville**

*This Ford, set up as a petroleum-hauling rig, was photographed in Puerto Rico in 1986.*

**1980s Ford L 9000**

*An L 9000 Model Ford is set up as a truck and trailer loaded with gasoline to deliver to Washington State. The rig is pulling for Bosman, Incorporated of Bellingham and Lynden, Washington.*

**1980s Ford 9000**

*Heavy earth-moving equipment is serviced in the field, thanks to this LTL 9000 Ford, circa 1984, which is set up as a bobtail, or straight-truck.*

> ## Not just a new Ford . . . a new Ford attitude.
> Ford brochure, 1991

**1980s Ford CL 9000**

*A CL 9000 is seen here pulling for Wheaton Van Lines of Indianapolis, Indiana. This tractor features a short drom box behind its cab. Extra payload space can be attained when the additional body of a drom unit is added to a tractor, resulting in more revenue.*

**1991 Ford AeroForce brochure**

## 1990s Ford

*This photo was taken in Twin Falls, Idaho, in 1994, and shows a "Two-Story Edsel" Ford cab-over pulling a set of "Rocky Mountain Doubles" for Rogers Seed Company.*

## 1990s Ford CL

*A CL Model Ford cab-over day cab, circa 1990, is seen here at an Anaheim, California, truck show. The CL Model was quite popular with truckers who ran both locally and long-distance.*

# Freightliner

## On-Going Innovation

**Above: 1970s White-Freightliner Powerliner**
*White-Freightliner came out with the Powerliner in the mid-1970s. It had a bigger radiator area, a larger windshield, and doors that could only fit other Powerliners. The model was only produced for a few years.*

**Left: 1942 Freightliner 600**
*This Freightliner conventional, fully restored, sits on display at an Anaheim, California, truck show, illustrating the earliest beginnings of Freightliner's history.*

ompared to a lot of other truck makers, Freightliner might be considered the new kid on the block, as it officially got its start just before World War II. The company's roots go back to the 1930s, when Leland James, president of Consolidated Freightways of Spokane, Washington, was unhappy with the trucks that were being offered at that time and decided to do something about it. He determined that he would build his own trucks, in his own shops, with his own mechanics, and use more aluminum in his models in order to keep weight down and payload up—this he accomplished.

In 1939, a new truck was built in Salt Lake City, Utah, using lightweight aluminum, and a new enterprise, the Freightways Manufacturing Company, was born. The first Freightliner, called the CF-100, rolled out in 1940. Consolidated Freightways, the parent company to the Freightways Manufacturing Company, was set to market its new aluminum Class 8 truck, but World War II ultimately shut down production.

With World War II in full swing, another war was taking place between Consolidated Freightways and the federal government. The government had charged Consolidated Freightways and Freightways Manufacturing with restraint of trade and monopoly policies. As a result, both Freightliner and Freightways were broken up, which prompted a move from Salt Lake City to Portland, Oregon.

After the war overseas had ended, Freightliner returned in full swing, producing big rigs that were much lighter than those of its competition, thanks to a greater use of aluminum. In 1942, a conventional was built, called the Model 600, but it was the rounded "Bubblenose" Model 800 cab-over that really established Freightliner as a viable builder of Class 8 trucks. The introduction of the Bubblenose occurred after the company changed its name to the Freightliner Corporation in 1947.

In 1950, the Hyster Company of Portland, Oregon, bought one of Freightliner's first sleeper cab-overs, the Model 900. This original truck, after logging more than four million miles (6.4 million km), is now fully restored and sits in the Smithsonian Museum in Washington, D.C.

The White Motor Company took over the responsibility of both the sales and the service of Freightliner in 1951, and the nameplate was changed to reflect this. The truck was now called White-Freightliner, and over 100,000 of this new breed were sold in the United States and Canada. Many are still on the road today.

Around 1953, White-Freightliner became the first Class 8 truck maker to come out with a roof-mounted sleeper, often called the "Tiltin' Hilton" due to the rocking that occurred when the truck was in motion. This sleeper was very important to truckers out West using truck and trailer configurations where load space was critical, especially in loading animals for livestock transportation.

The first tilting cab-over by White-Freightliner took to the highways around 1958. This innovation allowed the entire cab to be tilted forward so that the engine could be accessed for repairs.

In 1960, the company produced the Model WFT-7242, with a 72-inch (183-cm) sleeper cab. This model was ideal for truck and trailer operators or for semis that needed shorter wheelbases, as length laws in the 1940s through the 1960s were quite restrictive in each of the forty-eight contiguous states. In 1974, White-Freightliner came out with a conventional truck, the WFT-8164, and many of its parts were interchangeable with its sister cab-over model, the WFT-7242.

Shortly after making the new conventional, White-Freightliner came out with a cab-over called the Powerliner, which looked much like the company's other cab-overs, except that it had a massive grille area and a slightly wider windshield. The large grille was to accommodate the V-12 Detroit Diesel engines that powered the trucks, though many of the Powerliners used smaller Cummins, Caterpillar, or Detroit Diesel engines. The Powerliner was only made for a short time before being discontinued and is a rare sight to see today.

In 1981, Daimler-Benz AG of Stuttgart, Germany, which was later merged to form DaimlerChrysler AG, bought White-Freightliner, and sales continued to grow. In 1992, their sales controlled almost 24 percent of all Class 8 sales. Freightliner in turn acquired Ford's remaining stock of Class 8 trucks in the late 1990s and became the parent company of the new Sterling line of trucks that came out in 1998. In 2000, Freightliner purchased Detroit Diesel as well as Western Star, which continues to operate independently.

Freightliner's continued success can be partly credited to its aggressive sales program, as the company will often do whatever it takes to get a trucker into one of their rigs. Case in point: A trucker driving for Bekins Van Lines of Hillside, Illinois, was returning to Seattle after dropping off a shipment in Los Angeles. Upon arriving in Bakersfield, California, he found that he needed to replace a headlight on his vintage 1954 Kenworth cab-over and went into the Freightliner store to get a new one. Not only did the trucker come out with a new headlight, but he also walked out with a new Freightliner! That same driver has since replaced his original Freightliner with another new Freightliner, running Seattle to New York for United Van Lines of Fenton, Missouri (and oh yes, he still has his old KW!). With this kind of sales success, it's no wonder that we see more and more Freightliners on our Interstates.

**1951 White-Freightliner**
*Showcased at a 1990s truck show is a White-Freightliner sleeper-cab tractor. This rig is the pride and joy of Market Transport of Portland, Oregon.*

*Top right:* **1948 Freightliner advertisement**

*Bottom right:* **1950s Buda engine advertisement**

**1950s White-Freightliner brochure**

**1960s White-Freightliner WFT 7242**
*This White-Freightliner, which hails from Eugene, Oregon, was spotted at the Martinez Truck Stop on Alameda Street in Los Angeles. Truck and trailer rigs like this one were quite popular on the West Coast from the 1940s into the 1960s.*

**1960s White-Freightliner**
*Cattle rode in style when they rode in this purple White-Freightliner truck and trailer rig, circa 1966, that pulled for the Fresno Meat Company of Fresno, California.*

**1960s White-Freightliner**
*Funderburk Trucking checks the weight of their White-Freightliner at the scales of Jerrell's Truck Plaza in Doswell, Virginia, in this 1967 photo.*

**1965 White-Freightliner**
*White-Freightliners became a popular truck for the nation's cross-country van line operators, as this 1968 photograph shows. Shown in the background is another favorite truck, the International Emeryville.*

**1969 White-Freightliner**
*The "Tiltin' Hilton" penthouse sleeper mounted above the driver of this 1969 White-Freightliner moving truck allows for the addition of a drom box behind the cab, providing extra payload space for this Iowa-based bedbug hauler.*

**1971 White-Freightliner**
*Originally this White-Freightliner was just another tractor in the Los Angeles fleet of Ralphs Grocery trucks. The unit was eventually converted into a mobile generator truck for the motion-picture industry.*

**1980s Freightliner**
*Check out the wheelbase of this Freightliner, with its set of milk-tank trailers! Souza Milk Transport of Gustine, California, owns this clean cab-over.*

**1980s Freightliner**

*In addition to its regular sleeper, this Freightliner, circa 1988, has a LivLab sleeper. The LivLab could offer just about anything that a trucker would need in the way of amenities, including a stove, shower, microwave, TV, or computer, as well as generous storage space and a large bunk area.*

**1980s Freightliner**

*An example of an odd configuration, this Freightliner can carry an automobile atop its cab and still have room for a drom box behind the sleeper.*

**1980s Freightliner**

*This rather strange-looking Freightliner cab-over was photographed in British Columbia, hauling wood products. Truck and trailer combinations can be different in other countries.*

**1991 Freightliner**
*Wayne Willnauer of Gilroy, California, trains, sells, shows, and transports horses with the aid of this Freightliner. The drom box is used for storing extra equipment for his four-legged cargo.*

**1990s Freightliner**
*Creech Brothers Horse Transportation of Troy, Missouri, owns this neat-looking Freightliner, circa 1990. Horse-haulers are a special breed of trucker, and many of their trucks are unique as well. Their trailers are custom-made to provide a safe ride for their cargo and can often cost as much, if not more, than the tractors that pull them.*

**1990s Freightliner FLD**
*Entire books could be published just on the great-looking trucks that only haul race cars. The Freightliner seen here is run by the Fugowie Racing Team, which was named after a lost Native American tribe.*

**1990s Freightliner**
*Freightliner is famous for building the unusual, like this low-mount truck with twin set-back steering axles. This unit is used for pumping concrete in high-rise applications.*

**1990s Freightliner XL**
*The long-hood XL shown here in Pennsylvania, is the favorite for individual truckers and fleets that wish to maintain high driver morale. "Large cars" may not get the best fuel mileage, but they sure get the attention of other truckers and motorists.*

**1990s Freightliner FLDs**
*The two Freightliners seen here are part of a much larger fleet of trucks that haul bulk cement and other related commodities into California, Arizona, Nevada, and Utah for Kitchens Transport of Victorville, California. These two rigs pull "powder train trailers," which haul powdered cement and are a common sight out West.*

**2000 Freightliner Argosy**
*Freightliner is one of the last truck makers that still sees the need for a contemporary cab-over model. Their latest entry in the cab-over market is the Argosy. This photograph was taken at a Fresno Truck Center, a large Freightliner dealer that has sales and service facilities all over Central California.*

**1990s Freightliner**
*The trucks from Double Eagle Trucking of Hesperia, California, grab everyone's attention when their powder trains run down the Interstates of California and Nevada. This truck was built around 1996.*

# GMC

## Consistent Quality

*Above:* **1962 GMC brochure**

*Left:* **1947 GMC A**
*An A Model GMC sits in the rain in Irwindale, California. This "Jimmy" ran from Los Angeles, California, to Phoenix, Arizona, hauling produce for Bob Pielemeier of Arcadia, California.*

General Motors is one of the largest corporations in the world today, having over 400,000 employees in over seventy-three countries. However, like most enterprises with roots going back to the early 1900s, GM came from humble beginnings. The company got its start in Michigan in a crude machine shop as a joint venture between brothers Max and Morris Grabowsky and saloon keepers Barney Finn and Albert Marx. GM was then known as the Rapid Motor Vehicle Company, but when William C. Durant took over operations around 1908, the name was changed to the General Motors Company. By 1911, it was known as the General Motors Truck and Coach Division, with its operations based in Pontiac, Michigan.

Like others building cars and trucks when World War I broke out, GM was called upon to supply the military with the motorized vehicles necessary to win the war. GM answered this call, and after the war, the company went on to become a successful builder of trucks for civilian use as well.

During the 1920s, GMCs came in various sizes with many applications, but they were not offered as Class 8 trucks until 1931, when the T-95 came into the picture. The T-95 was a three-axle rig equipped with air brakes and a four-speed transmission and could handle payloads up to 30,000 pounds (13,620 kg).

The Great Depression took its toll on GM, but it was able to survive the lean years by building its own line of trailers in addition to making trucks. Its trailers were sold for both city and rural use. GM's progress continued, and in 1934, it debuted its first cab-over model. Sleepers were now also offered as an option.

By 1939, GMC had introduced its famous A Model. Some in trucking say that the long-hooded A Models were the best-looking truck GM ever produced—and when coupled with a 671 "Screaming Jimmy," the Detroit Diesel engine that was most often found in the GMC trucks of the 1940s through the 1980s, it was music to your ears!

When World War II broke out, GMC was there to offer many different models to the military. They included three-axle troop transport trucks, jeeps, ambulances, and the famous DUKW amphibious "Duck," which was used to transport troops and equipment across both water and land.

The A Model was still in production after the war and was a favorite of truckers up until 1949, as this truly was a Class 8 truck with a lot of "class." But in 1949, a new truck called the H Model, which was also referred to as GMC's 900 Series, replaced the A Model. This truck featured a larger rounded cab, a larger two-piece windshield, and a much lower running board.

A sister truck would soon follow the H Model in the form of a cab-over, often called the "Cannonball." The rig's integral sleeper, which came as an option, was quite small to say the least—less than 36 inches (91 cm) wide—but if you were tired, anything was better than nothing! The Cannonball was made until 1959, eventually giving way to the "Crackerbox" cab-over.

While the Crackerbox was being made prior to the discontinuance of the Cannonball, it wasn't really visible on the trucking scene until around 1960. The Crackerbox cab-over was a square, no-frills truck, but with a sleeper cab and a fair amount of chrome, it wasn't a bad-looking rig to see going down the Interstate. The Crackerbox was widely acclaimed on both sides of the country, as many steel haulers, freight lines, and van lines, or "bedbug haulers," liked this particular rig. They appreciated the model's strong, simple construction, its use of chrome, and the fact that parts replacement was comparatively easy.

In 1968, the Crackerbox was replaced by the Astro 95, which was an all new design for GMC with rounded lines and a larger windshield. Later models of this cab-over had a radiator area large enough to handle the mighty V-12 engines offered by Detroit Diesel, part of the GM family.

The H Models of the '50s and '60s gave way to the 9500 Series Brigadier, a conventional with a long, tilting fiberglass hood. This extended hood could easily hold any size Detroit Diesel, Cummins, or Caterpillar engine at that time. The stately Brigadier eventually stepped aside for the next generation of conventionals. The General, which was a twin to the Chevrolet Bison, was introduced as the Brigadier's successor in the early 1970s.

Although GMC continues to build smaller Class 7 and under rigs, the company no longer makes its own Class 8 trucks. GMCs were made until 1988, when they became part of the Volvo-White family of trucks. The conglomerate included Volvo, White, GMC, and Autocar, and was renamed the Volvo GM Heavy Truck Corporation.

Today, one can see GMC's name alongside Volvo-White's on Class 8 big rigs, but there was a time, not so very long ago, that the nameplate of GMC stood proudly by itself as a leader in the Class 8 truck industry.

**1940s GMC**
*Colors for this GMC cab-over were light cream and dark blue. Helms Bakery ran this truck and trailer from their Culver City, California, plant to their Montebello, California, facility, hauling the products that made their pastries famous.*

> **When you buy a GMC for heavy hauling you get a truck that's heavy duty and all truck.**
> GMC ad, 1948

**On Battle Lines or Transport Lines –**

**–the GMCs are out in front**

General Motors Trucks and Coaches are pulling the most important loads in their history. Where our fighting forces depend on power, speed and flexibility—you'll find more GMCs than any other make of heavy military truck. GMC factories have more than doubled their output, to keep our Army out in front in motorized transportation. Along our nation-wide war-production lines, the GMCs are helping to provide the quickest transportation the world has ever seen. In countless war-manufacturing areas, vast fleets of GMC-built Yellow Coaches are delivering the workers to their vital jobs. In the Army and on the highway, the GMCs are working over-time for victory.

Better-serviced trucks serve America better! Investigate "Victory Maintenance"—GMC's answer to war-time needs for peak performance, economy and longer truck life. This truck saving program is available for trucks of all makes, through GMC Branches and Dealers in every section of the country.

**VICTORY MAINTENANCE**
KEEP 'EM ROLLING FOR THE JOB

**GENERAL MOTORS TRUCK & COACH**
DIVISION OF YELLOW TRUCK & COACH MANUFACTURING COMPANY
Home of GMC Trucks and Yellow Coaches • • Manufacturer of a Wide Variety of Military Vehicles for our Armed Forces

**WWII GMC advertisement**

**1948 GMC A**

*Terry Fortier's restored 1948 A Model GMC is partnered with a 35-foot (10.7-m) freight trailer from the same era in this photo taken in Fresno, California.*

**1948 GMC advertisement**

**1950s GMC 900**

*In this 1957 photograph, we see a dark green GMC 900 Series set up as a truck and trailer lumber rig. Notice that there are only two marker lights on the roof of the cab; the requirement of five marker lights did not become a federal law until the early 1960s.*

**1950s GMC Cannonball**

*A GMC Cannonball with an integral sleeper is seen in this 1965 photo, which was taken near Toledo, Ohio. Murphy Transportation of Hampton, Iowa, ran a fleet of GMCs, hauling refrigerated commodities as well as livestock. Their colors were light green and white.*

**GMC** DIESEL **D920-67**

## Powered by the Famed GM "6-71" Diesel

This rugged engine packs the kind of brawny, low-cost power that makes GMC Series 920 tractors No. 1 choice for heavyweight Diesel hauling up to 65,000 pounds GCW!

Rugged operations—on or off-the-highway—get extra drive and stamina from GMC's exclusive 2-cycle engine design which delivers sustained, faster-accelerating power with every downstroke of every piston! Other power-producing features include triple-cooled pistons, Uniflow scavenging, direct fuel injection and performance-proved engineering throughout.

**1953 GMC D920-67 brochure**

**1950s GMC 860**
*Seaway Foods of Cleveland, Ohio, ran this 860 Series GMC, circa 1958. The single-axle tractor seen in this photo from 1965 is hooked to a 40-foot (12.2-m) trailer.*

**1950s GMC 860**
*Schwartz Brothers Van & Storage of Chicago, Illinois, hauled household goods with this GMC, circa 1953, well into the 1960s, as agents for Allied Van Lines. The trailer was 35 feet (10.7 m) in length.*

**1953 GMC D 660-47 brochure**

**1955 GMC 370 brochure**

**1960s GMC**

*This 1965 photograph shows one of the GMCs that the Mary Carter Paint Company of Matawan, New Jersey, ran coast-to-coast. The Mary Carter fleet of GMCs could be seen in most parts of the country.*

**1950s GMC Cannonball**

*The pride of Frank Costa's fleet of "bullwagons," or livestock trucks, was this late-1950s, two-tone blue GMC cab-over. Costa ran a mixed fleet of livestock rigs and was based in Artesia, California.*

**1960s GMC Crackerbox**

*Bontrager Truck Service of Goshen, Indiana, ran this red Crackerbox, circa 1960, out West every week. Notice the set-back front axle on this tractor.*

**1966 GMC Crackerbox**
*To commemorate the fiftieth anniversary of the first transcontinental run by a GMC truck, GMC brought out this Crackerbox cab-over called the "Golden Pacemaker." It was later repainted a bright red and hauled goods in the Los Angeles area for Carnation Dairy Products.*

**1960s GMC Brigadier**
*Pacific Concrete of Honolulu, Hawaii, ran this long-hood GMC, circa 1966, as a cement-mixer. This truck was meant to work in severe environments, so there is no chrome or "gingerbread" on the rig.*

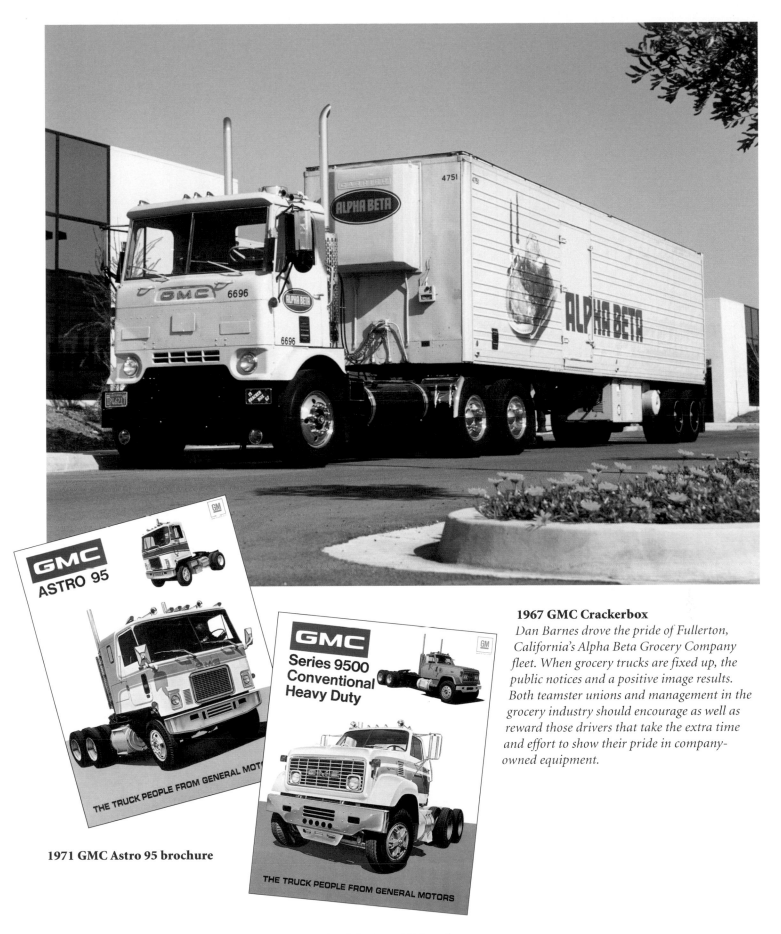

**1967 GMC Crackerbox**
*Dan Barnes drove the pride of Fullerton, California's Alpha Beta Grocery Company fleet. When grocery trucks are fixed up, the public notices and a positive image results. Both teamster unions and management in the grocery industry should encourage as well as reward those drivers that take the extra time and effort to show their pride in company-owned equipment.*

1971 GMC Astro 95 brochure

1971 GMC Series 9500 brochure

**1980s GMC General**

*This GMC, circa 1980, was leased to an automobile transport company and owned by a trucker from Pennsylvania when this photograph was taken in 1988.*

**1980s GMC**

*The GMC cab-over shown here has two sleepers—one is a standard sleeper cab, the other is located above the driver as a penthouse sleeper. The tractor was leased to Mitchell Trucking of LaPorte, Indiana.*

**1980s GMC General**

*Ratner Brothers ran this GMC General in the 1980s. Unlike its "twin," the Chevy Titan, the General was well received by those in trucking.*

**1980s GMC**
*A late-1980s GMC cab-over is parked at a Las Vegas, Nevada, truck stop. The larger radiator area on this truck replaced the smaller one that first made its appearance in the 1968 debut of GMC's Astro 95.*

# International

## *Meeting World Challenges*

**Above: 1950s International Cherrypicker**
*Owen C. Glass of North Little Rock, Arkansas, ran this Cherrypicker to the West Coast every week. The trailer is a 40-foot (12.2-m) reefer.*

**Left: 1998 International 9300**
*R&K Trucking of Casper, Wyoming, owns this International, which is being loaded with lumber in Ogden, Utah.*

International Harvester, renamed the Navistar International Transportation Corporation in 1986, has roots that go back to the 1830s, when founder Cyrus Hall McCormick spent countless hours tinkering with the farming implements on his family's Virginia homestead and ultimately developed the farm tractor.

Since International Harvester's official formation in 1902, much has happened to the Chicago-based company, as they have gone on to build farm equipment, refrigeration units, and all sorts of trucks—from pickups to large off-highway models that the motoring public seldom sees. This chapter is going to cut across most of IH's early history and deal with their entry into the Class 8 market of trucks.

Like most other truck builders, International eased its way into the Class 8 arena in the late 1920s. It offered two-speed rear axles in its 1928 models, which featured a prototypical diesel engine. In the early 1930s, an optional sleeper cab became available, and in 1934, International took on the art deco look popular at that time with a more rounded and streamlined cab.

"Cornbinders," as International trucks were called, continued to be a popular rig throughout the 1930s, and as the decade drew to a close, the famous K Model made its debut. The K Model resembled IH's earlier D Model, as it had the same basic cab, but the K's lines were a bit more aerodynamic and cleaner in appearance. The K also had headlights that were lower and closer to the front bumper.

International Harvester built around 100,000 military vehicles in World War II, and many of these trucks saw civilian use after the war. By the war's end, IH had become the third-ranking truck maker in the United States with sales and factory branches in all parts of the world.

In 1946, the K Model was transformed into the KB, which was a little larger and had a front grille that extended over the lower fenders. A face-lift was in order for International's smaller trucks as well.

In 1947, a new IH factory opened up in Emeryville, California, and came out with a truck for western operators. This rig was called the Westcoaster and was offered either as a conventional or as a cab-over with a sleeper as an option. A variety of engines, transmissions, and wheelbases were available with this unit. Westcoasters were made up to 1949, with the K Series also ending about that same time.

Big changes were in store for IH in 1950 with the advent of the L and the R Series of trucks. The RDF Model was especially popular for truckers out West. It featured the new Comfo-Vision cab, which had a one-piece semi-curved windshield. The Comfo-Vision cabs used by IH were made by the Chicago Manufacturing Company and were also popular with other truck makers, such as Diamond T and Hendrickson, who incorporated this style into their own cabs.

The LCD-405 "Cherrypicker" cab-over, which was unleashed by International around 1953, was tall and narrow and looked quite impressive when it had a sleeper cab. The conventionals of this era also came with an integral sleeper, but it was the Cherrypicker that was the rig of choice for long-distance truckers, since the cab-over made it easier to comply with state length laws.

The "Highbinder" Emeryville cab-over of the late 1950s was a new concept in cab-overs for IH, as it had a two-piece flat windshield and was offered both as a day cab or sleeper cab, making it the choice for many of the decade's van lines. A companion model, called the DC, also came out at this time and was known as the "Donald Duck" International because of its strange appearance. This model, which was produced into the 1970s, was a common rig to see at construction sites.

In 1965, the last of the Emeryvilles were made. They were replaced by the CO-4000, which had an entirely new style to it and would set the trend for future International cab-overs. It had a semi-rounded two-piece windshield, rather than the two-piece flat windshields of the Emeryvilles, a newly designed cab, new doors, and a new grille. By 1974, the name "Transtar" was seen on the nameplates of IH 4000 Series trucks and became part of the vocabulary of the business.

All seemed to be going well for the corporation, until the next decade rolled in. A strike that lasted from 1979 to 1980 had a negative impact on production throughout the company, and the farm crisis of 1980, which sent agricultural sales downward, had an adverse effect on IH as well. If that were not enough, tougher federal mandates concerning cleaner-burning engines brought International to its knees.

They were down, but definitely not out—in February 1986, IH divested itself of its farming machinery division and the International Harvester name, selling them to the Case Corporation of Racine, Wisconsin, through Case's parent company, Tenneco, Incorporated. After the sale, International officially changed its name to Navistar International and adorned its trucks with a new, more contemporary logo.

A big burden had been lifted from the company, and it could now rededicate itself to the making of Class 7 and 8 trucks, school buses, and fire-fighting equipment, as well as engines. Navistar International, like Mack Trucks, continues to make its own engines, in addition to offering outside vendor components from Cummins, Caterpillar, and Detroit Diesel. For its mid-range diesels, Navistar currently makes engines with ratings from 160 to 300 hp.

In addition to being a leader in both school bus and fire engine production, Navistar International is a major builder of an on- or off-highway truck called the Paystar, a machine designed to take on a world of punishment in hostile environments. The Paystar's many applications include oil field use, hauling raw sugar cane, and the movement of assembled building structures.

In March 1999, the company phased out all domestic production of their Class 8 cab-overs, thus joining Mack, Ford, and others in making only conventional trucks because of the more liberal length laws that now exist.

The conventional International Eagle 9900 Series, which was first introduced in the late 1970s, is still going strong today. It is a Class 8 truck popular with truckers who want to be noticed. With its long hood, generous amount of chrome, and smooth lines, this truck has no problem winning the affection of even the most die-hard Peterbilt owner!

The 9900ix was brought out in 1999, and is the flagship of Navistar International. It is designed for the long-distance trucker, having all the amenities that one could ask for, as well as being dipped in chrome. This rig is for the trucker who wants to make the statement that he or she has truly arrived.

While International may have had problems in the past, this company has proven, much to the amazement of many people, that adversity may sometimes be a blessing in disguise. Today Navistar International is very much alive and well. With over forty plant locations and more than 17,000 employees, the company is poised for the new millennium and the challenges that are sure to go with it.

**1940s International K**
*An unrestored 1940s K Model International is seen here on display at an antique truck show in Tukwila, Washington.*

**1940s International Westcoaster**

*An International Westcoaster cab-over, circa 1947, is set to haul cattle across Southern California in this 1956 photograph.*

**1940s International Westcoaster**

*This International Westcoaster, circa 1948, was owned by Davies Trucking of Montebello, California. Note that the truck still has a turn signal arm behind the driver's door; by the late 1950s, manually operated turn signal arms had been phased out by directional lights.*

*Top left:* **1940 International advertisement**

*Middle left:* **1945 International advertisement**

*Bottom left:* **1954 International 400 Series brochure**

### 1950s International Cherrypicker

*This Cherrypicker, circa 1956, has both a sleeper and a drom combination. W. L. Davis leased this dark blue cab-over to Sinclair Produce of Glascow, Montana. The photo was taken at a yard owned by Joe Cabral of Montebello, California.*

### 1957 International Cherrypicker

*This photograph shows a Cherrypicker with a set of doubles pulling for Garibaldi Brothers Livestock Transportation of Maywood, California. Notice the sheep baskets under each of the two trailers that allowed for more payload to be carried.*

### 1950s International RD

*A late-1950s International pulls its weight, as it cruises down a Honolulu freeway in 1974. There is not much demand for a truck with a sleeper in Hawaii, as all trucking is local.*

### 1950s International R

*An R Model with a set-back front axle is seen here, leased to B&P Motor Express of Pittsburgh, Pennsylvania. There is a small Mercury sleeper on this steel-hauling rig, which was produced by Mercury Fabricators of Cudahy, California.*

**1950s International R 200**
*An R 200 Model with a factory sleeper poses for its picture at an Oregon antique truck show.*

**1963 International brochure**

**1960s International Emeryville**
*This grain hauler, circa 1961, is parked at a truck stop in Colton, California. Though it had a day-cab, this rig was most likely used as a sleeper—affording very little room for tired drivers.*

### 1964 International Emeryville
*An Emeryville with a day-cab is shown here, pulling for Valley Motor Lines, of Fresno, California, which later became part of the Valley-Copperstate-Pierce and Sunset Motor Lines conglomerate. The new company had operating authority from the Pacific Northwest into the Southwest long before deregulation was implemented.*

### *Above:* 1965 International DC
*Taken at Mike & Vic's Truck Stop in North Lima, Ohio, in 1965, this "Donald Duck" International had a rare integral sleeper cab; most rigs of this model had no sleepers, as they were set up to run locally.*

### *Right:* 1965 International Emeryville
*This Emeryville with integral sleeper was photographed in Fresno, California in 1967. The tractor pulled doubles for Los Angeles Seattle Motor Express (LASME), running the entire West Coast.*

**1970s International Transtar Eagle**
*This Transtar Eagle, circa 1979, runs from Los Angeles to Las Vegas, pulling a set of pneumatic trailers, or powder trains.*

**1980s International**
*Here is proof that there was at least one International that sported a 110-inch (279-cm) cab! This unit, circa 1980, was trip-leased to the steel-hauling division of Yellow Freight System, who has freight terminals all across the country with headquarters located in Overland Park, Kansas.*

**1980s International**
*This sharp-looking cab-over wore a coat of deep metallic blue paint and was a contestant at a Santa Ana, California, truck show in the 1980s.*

**1980s International**

*Las Vegas, Nevada, has been called "The City That Never Sleeps," partly because construction is an on-going event. This International supplies cement to the many construction sites located in the city that reinvents itself every few years.*

**1980s International S 2200**

*A clean S 2200 Model, circa 1986, sits on display at a Pomona, California, truck show. This particular model is quite popular for making local pick ups and deliveries.*

**1990s International 9700**

*An International, circa 1995, with a set-back front axle runs coast-to-coast hauling household goods for Big John's Moving and Storage of New York City.*

**1998 International 9200**
*This neat-looking petroleum hauler, owned by Fredericksen Tank Lines of West Sacramento, California, is seen at a North Las Vegas, Nevada, refinery.*

*Above:* **2000 International 9900s**
*Three Model 9900 tractors await their lucky new owners at the McCandless International Truck dealership in Las Vegas, Nevada.*

*Left:* **1998 International Paystar 5000**
*A mighty Paystar 5000 sits on the beach in Santa Monica, California. This truck uses both CNG (compressed natural gas) and diesel fuel to operate. The City of Santa Monica owns this truck, which is used to maintain its beach.*

**1999 International 2674**
*This International is one of three such water tenders that supply other fire trucks with water when they fight the dangerous brush and canyon blazes that plague Los Angeles County nearly every year. It is a 6x6 Caterpillar-powered truck with an Allison automatic transmission.*

# Kenworth

## Changing with the Times

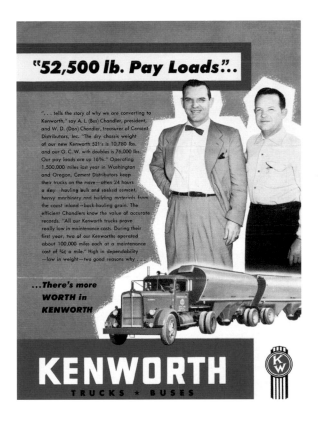

*Above:* **1950s Kenworth advertisement**

*Left:* **1950s Kenworth C525**
*Don Wayne of Las Vegas, Nevada, operating as Cal-Nev Produce, ran this butterfly-hood Kenworth between Las Vegas and Los Angeles several times a week in the 1980s.*

There is a certain mystique that goes along with owning or driving a Kenworth. Some call this truck the "Cadillac" of Class 8 trucks, and sales in both new and used Kenworths reflect this.

Kenworth, like a few other makes, was born out of necessity—to move logs and timber for the forest industry in the Northwest. The company began in 1915 as the Gerlinger Manufacturing Company of Portland, Oregon, and migrated to Seattle, Washington, two years later. In 1923, its name was changed to the Kenworth Truck Company in a tribute to two of its largest stockholders, G. W. Kent and E. K. Worthington.

During the 1920s, Kenworth made various sizes of trucks, from 1½- to 5-ton (1.4 to 4.5-t) units, with engines that were usually four-cylinder Budas, quite a common engine for that time, produced by the Buda Division of the Allis-Chalmers Manufacturing Company of Harvey, Illinois. In 1927, KW used a 78-hp six-cylinder engine, and by 1932, it was one of the first truck makers to offer a diesel engine as an option.

In its early days, Kenworth was a regional truck, primarily designed for use along the West Coast. Besides providing quality trucks to the area, Kenworth was also making both buses and fire-fighting apparatus. To have a KW fire engine parked inside your fire station meant that you had the finest in equipment.

In 1935, the traditional chrome grille made its appearance. The first chromed grilles were referred to as "shovel-noses" due to their shape, but they soon evolved into a more conservative look from the 1940s into the 1960s.

Like the rest of the trucking industry, Kenworth did its part in World War II, building tanks and wreckers for the military in the early 1940s. Before the war ended, KW became part of Pacific Car and Foundry, joining its ranks in 1944.

Upon completion of World War II, KW resumed building civilian Class 8 trucks, both as conventional and cab-over models. Sales were starting to climb, and Kenworth was the truck to own and/or drive, especially for truckers out West. Kenworth cab-overs were always a popular model, from their inception before the war through the 1940s and 1950s. Cab sizes generally ran from 63 inches (160 cm), to the later 110-inch (279-cm) sleeper models that were so popular in the 1970s, to the even more modern 86- to 110-inch (218- to 279-cm) Aerodyne models of the 1980s.

Around 1954, Kenworth and the Boeing Aircraft Company, also of Seattle, combined their skills and placed a gas turbine engine into a KW conventional, pulling for West Coast Fast Freight. Although this was only an experiment, it was a glimpse into what the future might hold. Also in 1954, Kenworth came out with the cab-beside-engine (CBE) model, but its lack of popularity ended production just a few years later.

The slightly squared "Bullnose" KW cab-overs that were produced from the late 1940s to 1956 gave way to the K Model cab-overs of the late 1950s. The Kenworth models of this era have stood the test of time—in comparing a 1957 Kenworth cab-over with a new Kenworth cab-over, it is evident that the basic style has remained unchanged, though more improvements, like the use of lighter-weight materials in cab construction and a slightly modernized grille and headlight design, have been made to the newer model.

By the late 1950s, Kenworth was offering a fiberglass tilting front hood for their conventionals as an option. The older butterfly hood, single headlight, and metal fenders could still be ordered, but the fiberglass tilt-hoods would be standard on all on-highway models by 1965.

One of the last years that the older-style conventional, which featured a small two-piece windshield, could be ordered was 1964, as the W Model became available that same year. This new-style cab had more room and a much larger two-piece windshield, bearing little resemblance to previous conventional models.

In the late 1960s and well into the 1980s, "large cars" or big trucks were "in." Trucks with long hoods were the rigs of choice for small fleets and individual truckers, and KW was there to oblige the demand. After 1984, the folks at KW decided to discontinue making these longer hoods. While Kenworth's sales began to drop, Peterbilt's sales of their long-hoods skyrocketed. By the beginning of the 1990s, however, Kenworth realized that it had made a mistake and reintroduced their long-hood conventionals with the W900L.

Because of a dramatic rise in fuel prices, Kenworth brought out the aerodynamic T-600 in 1985. This model was also known as the "Anteater," due to the distinctive sloping shape of its hood. The T-600 has been updated since its introduction to further increase fuel mileage, but unfortunately for truckers the cost of diesel fuel has enjoyed a steady increase as well.

The next generation of aerodynamic trucks by Kenworth, the T-2000, was introduced in the late 1990s. Many truckers call this model the "Dodge Ram on Steroids," because its rounded lines make it look like a beefed-up version of the Dodge pickup truck.

In addition to building on-highway trucks, KW continues to be a leader in making off-highway models designed to tackle the tough work of hauling logs, taking on the oil fields of the Middle East, and handling the down-and-dirty work of hauling sugar cane in the Philippines.

While United States plants can be found in Seattle, Washington; Chillicothe, Ohio; and Renton, Washington, Kenworths are also made in Mexico, Canada, and Australia. Owning and/or driving a KW has always been a kind of status symbol, and today this mystique continues around the world.

**1940s Kenworth**
*This low-mount KW cattle truck was photographed at the Los Angeles Union Stockyards in 1956. Mouldner Livestock Transportation, based in Glendale, Arizona, ran a fleet of bullwagons in the Southwest in the '50s and '60s.*

**There's more worth in Kenworth.**
Company motto

**1950s Kenworth**
*The Bullnose Kenworth cab-over in this photo ran the eleven western states for Allan Arthur Livestock Transportation of Montebello, California. The company's mixed fleet of livestock trucks ran until February 1964, when the "corral" finally closed for this outfit.*

**1950s Kenworth**

*In 1954, Kenworth came out with the CBE (cab-beside-engine) model, which was produced for only a few years—it wasn't KW's most popular model.*

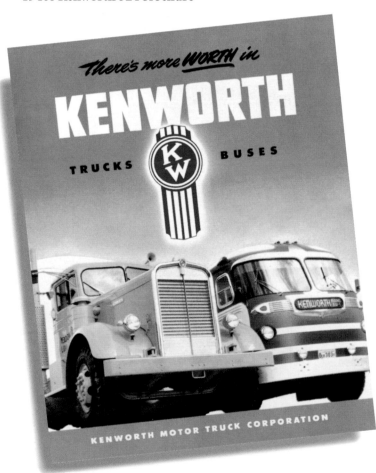

**1940s Kenworth 524 brochure**

**1940s Kenworth advertisement**

**1954 Kenworth**

*Question: How do you drop a twelve-cylinder Detroit Diesel engine into a 1954 KW conventional? Answer: Move the cab back one foot and extend the hood forward one foot. With the addition of two extra feet, you now have room for the engine, as is illustrated by this older Kenworth. This rig also distinguishes itself from other KWs by sporting Peterbilt headlights.*

**Opposite page: 1956 Kenworth**

*This neat-looking KW was restored and driven every day by Doug Main of Fillmore, California. The tractor pulled a flatbed trailer, which was used to haul concrete light poles.*

**1958 Kenworth**

*This photo, taken in Colton, California, in 1966, shows brothers Larry and Terry Klenske's two-tone metallic green KW conventional. The first year that factory dual headlights were available was 1958.*

**1950s Kenworth**

*Clifford Stubbs of Provo, Utah, ran this dark blue KW and 40-foot (12.2-m) American reefer trailer to Los Angeles in the '50s and '60s.*

**1950s Kenworth 521**
*For a few years in the late 1950s, Kenworth produced this interim model cab-over, after phasing out the famous Bullnose of the early 1950s.*

*Left:* **1950s Kenworth advertisement**

*Right:* **1950s Kenworth brochure**

**1950s Kenworth**

*Sitting on the Bandini Boulevard scales in Vernon, California, a Roscoe Wagner combination produce truck/bullwagon, circa 1958, prepares to deliver its load of cattle into the Los Angeles Union Stockyards. Started in Twin Falls, Idaho, in 1935, the Roscoe Wagner fleet of trucks can still be seen hauling livestock and produce throughout the West, and is also a successful dealer of trailers from the Wilson Trailer Company of Sioux City, Iowa.*

**1950s Kenworth**

*This Kenworth tanker, circa 1959, hauled acid for the Chipman Truck Company of Los Angeles. The KW parked behind this rig was one of many belonging to V. B. Morgan Tank Lines of Long Beach, California.*

**1963 Kenworth W925**

*The first of the wide-hood Kenworths featured a traditional smaller cab and windshield, which made this rig look very impressive going down the highway.*

**1965 Kenworth**

*Mike and Nita Massey of Terre Haute, Indiana, leased this 1965 318-hp Kenworth to Jekel Transfer and Storage of Grand Rapids, Michigan. Jekel was an agent for North American Van Lines of Fort Wayne, Indiana. This photo of North American's pride of the fleet was taken in 1966 at their West Coast yard in Pico Rivera, California.*

**1970 Kenworth Ks**

*Two new K Models pose side by side. B&G Trucking hauled steel in California and was based in Santa Fe Springs.*

**1974 Kenworth**

*This 1974 KW is a good example of what a small amount of chrome and a nice paint job can do for a truck's appearance. Combine these elements with a driver that maintains his or her truck, and you have a rig that looks like this!*

**1970s Kenworth**

*In the 1970s, in order to compete with White-Freightliner, Kenworth introduced the 110-inch (279-cm) sleeper cab-over, which was a favorite model for truckers who drove long distances. The truck shown here was built around 1978.*

**1970s Kenworth brochure**

**1980s Kenworth Aerodyne**

*From Corrales, New Mexico, comes this sharp-looking Aerodyne cab-over, circa 1980. Truckers favor the Aerodyne because it affords a greater amount of room in which to sleep.*

**1980s Kenworth**

*Kenworth scored a home run when it made the extended-hood model conventional, as is evident in this rig owned by Huff Trucking of Spanish Fork, Utah.*

**1980s Kenworth Brute**

*An early-1980s KW Brute, perfect for tough jobs, is seen as a dump truck in this photograph, which was taken in the East.*

**1980s Kenworth T-600**

*In 1985, Kenworth came out with its famous T-600, better known as the "Anteater." Miles Lane's Anteater is seen here running through some bad weather.*

**1980s Kenworth W900B**

*A W900B set up as a straight truck, circa 1986, is seen taking on a load of gasoline near Dawson Creek, British Columbia.*

**1994 Kenworth W900L**

*A clean-looking W900L pulling for R. C. Moore of Florida is shown here at a warehouse near Reno, Nevada, in 1994.*

**2000 Kenworth T-2000**
*The T-2000 is often referred to by many in trucking as the "Dodge Ram on Steroids." Fuel efficiency is said to have increased thanks to advanced designing in aerodynamics.*

**1998 Kenworth W900L**
*Another late-model W900L, this time set up as a truck and trailer, is owned by Cheyenne Rock Company of North Las Vegas, Nevada.*

**1999 Kenworth T-800**
*Although the massive T-800 shown here isn't completely hooked up to all of its trailers, this heavy hauler has been built to take on loads that cannot be carried by trucks that are specced out for on-highway use.*

# Mack

## The Bulldog Never Rests

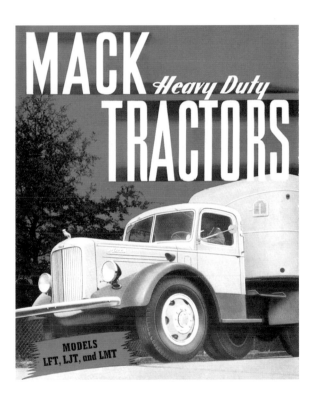

*Above:* **1944 Mack brochure**

*Left:* **1955 Mack LT**
*An LT poses long enough for this 1987 photo, taken in Las Vegas, Nevada. The LT Mack is considered by many in trucking to be the "Dusenberg of Diesels."*

Brooklyn, New York, was the starting point for brothers John and August Mack's venture into the truck-manufacturing industry in the 1890s. Back then the company was known as Mack Brothers Wagon Works, but this was changed to the International Motor Truck Corporation in 1916. Because many people confused the company with International Harvester, one of their chief rivals, it was renamed Mack Trucks, Incorporated in 1922.

Mack has a varied history as a "top dog" in the world of Class 8 trucks and a successful producer of both fire-fighting equipment and topnotch buses. The company was known to not only offer outside vendor engines and drive trains, but supply its own components as well. However, most people continue to associate the Mack Bulldog with an array of tough Class 8 trucks, and the phrase "built like a Mack truck" has become a part of every American's vocabulary.

As was the case with most established truck makers, Mack built various sizes of trucks from its inception. Also like most trucks from that era, Mack's models proved to be sturdy and reliable rigs that were instrumental in winning World War I.

In the 1920s, when others were focusing on smaller trucks, Mack was gearing up for the bigger rigs by coming out with a diesel-powered truck in 1927. Ten years later, they were offering their own brand of diesel engine in their rigs. During the war years of the 1940s, Mack built 35,000 trucks, and of these, 16,000 had Mack engines in them.

Prior to World War II, Mack brought out the L Model, and this truck was an instant success on both coasts. It had a square cab with rounded back corners and featured a large two-piece windshield. After the war, Mack revisited the L, making the LJ, the LF, and the LT, which by far stands out as the "Dusenberg of Diesels," with its long, stately hood, rounded fenders, and large, square, chromed radiator shell. Many of these can be seen at truck shows and often get the attention of even those who know nothing about trucks, due to the model's sharp appearance. Production of the LT ran for about ten years, ending around 1956. Some in trucking say that Mack should have never stopped making the LT, but rather updated it to have a more contemporary look.

The 1950s were indeed a productive decade for Mack. The company purchased Brockway Motor Trucks in 1956 and continued to offer a variety of their own models and an array of new Mack engines, transmissions, and rear-ends.

The W Model cab-over, brought out in 1953, looked similar to the Kenworth models of the time, and came as either a non-sleeper or sleeper, although the non-sleeper was more popular, especially when pulling a set of doubles on LTL or livestock runs.

The real hit of 1953 came in the form of the B Model Mack conventional. Most people in trucking will agree that this model was the most successful vehicle Mack Truck ever built. The B Model came in all sizes, from the smaller B-20 up to the B-87, and its rounded lines graced the cabs of many different types of trucks—from fire engines to heavy haulers to off-highway trucks that did logging and oil field work. All of these applications afforded the B Model a welcome place in trucking history.

That same year, the H Model "Cherrypicker" cab-over came out as the H-60 and H-61, which sat tall and proud as it made their way along the highways. The H Models of the early 1950s were especially popular in the eastern and southeastern part of the country, as companies like Riss International of Kansas City, Missouri, and Hennis Freight Lines of Winston-Salem, North Carolina, favored this truck. Around 1955, the H Model was scaled down as the H-63 but still retained the looks of the H-61. In the late 1950s, the H-67 came out, featuring dual headlights built into the fenders. The H-63 and H-67 Macks with sleeper cabs were especially popular with truckers who were pulling for the various van lines, hauling furniture cross-country. North American Van Lines of Fort Wayne, Indiana; Mayflower Transit of Carmel, Indiana; Allied Van Lines of Broadview, Illinois; and National Van Lines of Chicago, Illinois, all had many of these H Model Macks as part of their fleets.

After the H Model came the G Model in the late 1950s, which became a favorite among western operators. The G Model boasted outside door handles at the bottom of its doors, which allowed for easier entry.

In 1962, Mack introduced yet another new cab-over called the F Model, and it too scored a home run for Mack sales coast-to-coast. The F Models were built both in Allentown, Pennsylvania, and the company's newer factory in Hayward, California.

Not being content to sit back on its hind legs, in 1965 "The Bulldog" replaced the legendary B Model with its R Series conventional. From 1965 to 1987, various sizes of the R Model came out, including the Valu-Liner and the long-hooded Super-Liner. Some R Models are still in production today for use in the construction industry.

In the 1960s, Mack introduced the MB Model, which proved to be the right truck for city use and in the refuse and recycling industries. In the late 1970s, the MR replaced the MB Model with an entirely new look, and its low-entry cab made this an even more perfect cab-over for refuse hauling and for use in big cities, where heavy traffic made driving a Class 8 vehicle a challenge. Great for driving in congested areas where tight squeezes are a problem, the space-conscious MR is still being produced.

The year 1982 saw a new, more massive cab-over in the form of the MH Model. Like other cab-overs, it came either as a day cab or a sleeper cab. Later models looked a lot like the CL Models offered by Ford.

In 1987, Mack opened a brand new factory in Winnsboro, South Carolina, and with it came a new model, the CH. This truck was unlike any other Mack conventional. With its newly designed cab, more room was afforded to the driver, and its bold horizontal grille was pure Bulldog from the ground up.

As length laws became increasingly liberal throughout the country, more and more people began buying conventional trucks. Because of this dramatic rise in the popularity of conventionals, domestic production of Mack cab-overs ceased in 1994.

The Mack Vision was the company's last entry in the twentieth-century truck market, as it was introduced in 1999. Sporting sleek lines and an aerodynamic look, this breed of Mack should please most skeptics.

Although Mack had been affiliated with the French automaker Renault since the late 1970s, in 2000 the company was sold to Volvo Trucks North America of Greensboro, North Carolina. With capital from its new parent company, Mack Trucks promises more surprises and innovations as we go further into the new century. Look for greater improvements in Mack drivetrains and even more driver-friendly big rigs.

**1920s Mack brochure**

**Mack advertisement illustration**

**1940s Mack brochure**

**1950s Mack W**
*A W Model Mack, circa 1953, is seen here pulling a trailer that once belonged to Pacific Intermountain Express of Oakland, California. This photograph was taken at Mike & Vic's Truck Stop in Stoney Ridge, Ohio, in 1965.*

**1950s Mack LT**
*A restored LT Mack, circa 1955, sits in the shadows at an antique truck show held in Portland, Oregon. Some truckers think that Mack should never have discontinued this model, but instead refined and updated this attention-getter to make it look more contemporary.*

**1950s Mack H-63**
*Parked at a North American Van Lines terminal in Pico Rivera, California, is a H-63 Mack,* circa *1956, featuring a rather small sleeper.*

**1950s Mack H-61**
*The H-61 is a rare truck today, but there was a time in the 1950s when this Cherrypicker was a common sight, especially in the Southeast and the Midwest. The Mack shown here was built* circa *1953.*

**1950s Mack H Series brochure**

**1950s Mack H-67**

*The H-67 resembled the H-63, but the dual headlights that were built into the fenders differentiated this Mack from previous models. Leonard Brothers Transfer of Miami had a fleet of these Macks, which hauled aircraft parts from Florida to California.*

**1950s Mack G**

*Shown here is a G Model Mack, circa 1959, set up as a cattle truck. By its colors, the wood body appears to have once belonged to Frank V. Costa Livestock Transportation of Artesia, California.*

**1950s Mack B**

*The Cunningham Produce Company of Pompano Beach, Florida, ran this B Model Mack, circa 1959, from Florida to Ohio in the 1960s. The reliable workhorse is shown here in 1965.*

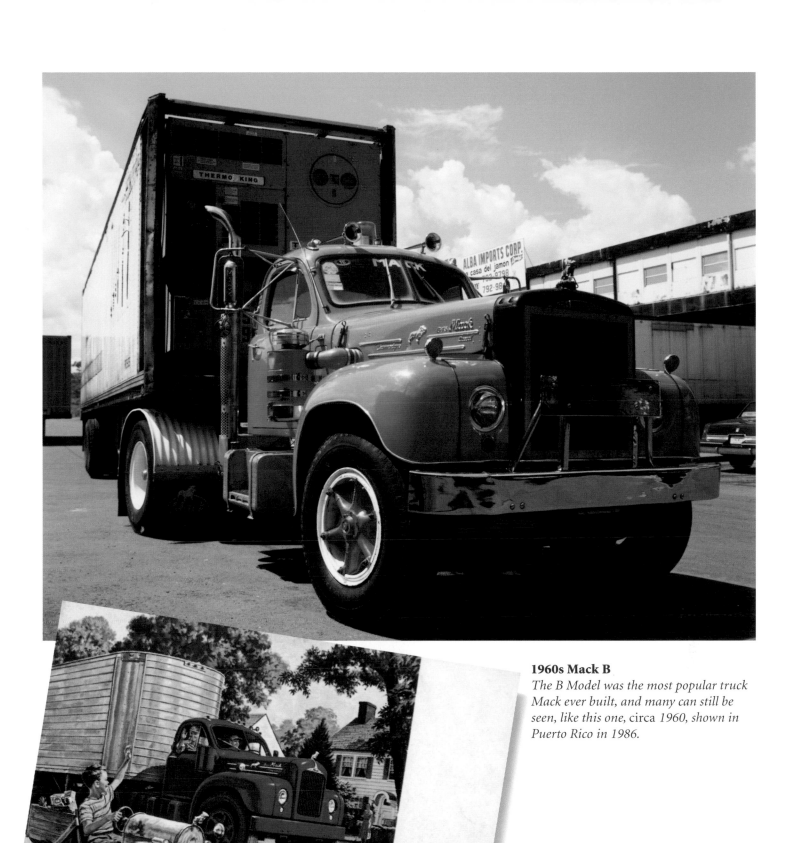

**1960s Mack B**
*The B Model was the most popular truck Mack ever built, and many can still be seen, like this one, circa 1960, shown in Puerto Rico in 1986.*

**1956 Mack brochure**

**1960 Mack G**

*Mack built the G Model beginning in the late 1950s for only a few years. The one shown here at the California-Arizona border in 1969 was owned by Jim Waldron; he leased this Mack to Boat Transit of Newport Beach, California.*

**1968 Mack R**

*An R Model Mack is delivering a load of gasoline to a Shell gas station in Covina, California.*

**1960s Mack F**

*This F Model Mack, circa 1963, is pulling a 40-foot (12.2-m) possum-belly Wilson livestock trailer for Geiger Brothers of Pandora, Ohio. The Mack F was a very popular model in the '60s.*

**1960s Mack FL**
*Ed C. Trimble hauled steel throughout California in the '60s and '70s with this sharp cab-over, circa 1969, which was made at Mack's Hayward, California, factory.*

**1976 Mack R Series brochure**

**1970s Mack FL**
*An FL Model Mack, wearing Peterbilt nameplates in jest, is seen in this photograph. The truck serves as a kind of mobile office for the Charlie Brown Construction Company of Las Vegas, Nevada.*

**1980s Mack Super-Liner**

*This Mack Super-Liner truck and trailer tanker rig hauled gasoline and diesel fuel from Oregon to Idaho. The Super-Liner was the last of Mack's long-hood breeds.*

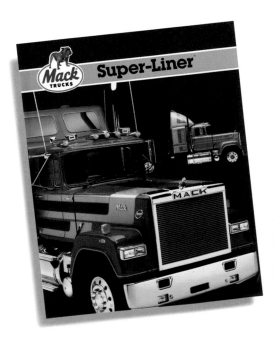

**1989 Mack Super-Liner brochure**

**1980s Mack MH**

*An MH Mack, circa 1980, proceeds across a Boston, Massachusetts, intersection in 1988. This model was very popular in the New England area.*

At home on the road, whatever the load.

Mack Super-Liner brochure, 1989

**1989 Mack MH**
*An impressive MH Model Mack is on display at a truck show in Anaheim, California. The MH was made until the early 1990s, when all domestic production of Mack cab-overs came to a halt.*

**1980s Mack Super-Liner**
*Truckers in New England love their Macks, and this Super-Liner is pure Bulldog. Bold striping and gold-leaf lettering is what sets this truck apart from the rest of the pack.*

**1997 Mack MR**

An MR Model Mack is seen here, working for Foothill Disposal, based in San Fernando Valley, California. The MR is a favorite among those in the refuse and recycling industries, as its low-entry cab makes climbing in and out of the truck much easier for the operator.

**1990s Mack CH**

Max Binswanger has been in the trucking business for over fifty years, hauling cement and building materials. His current fleet consists of CH Model Macks that run from California to Nevada.

**1998 Mack CH**

This CH Model, set up as a transfer-dump, is owned by 7 Counties Sand and Gravel Company of Colton, California. The gold, rather than chrome-plated, Bulldog on the hood indicates that this is a pure-bred Mack—the complete drivetrain (engine, transmission, and rear end) was produced entirely by Mack itself rather than outside vendors.

**2000 Mack Visions**

*The Mack Vision has entered the twenty-first century with a bold new look and promises to be a favorite with truckers across the country.*

# Marmon

## *Its Legend Lives On*

**Above: 1960s Marmon**
*L. E. Bradley of Texas pulled a 40-foot (12.2-m) refrigerated trailer to California with this Marmon cab-over in the early 1960s.*

**Left: 1990s Marmon**
*Neil's Auto Transport of North Salt Lake, Utah, hauls cars in the West with this Marmon. This photo was taken in Las Vegas, Nevada.*

The Marmon Motor Company got its start in Indianapolis, Indiana, in 1904 as an automobile manufacturer. Marmon was a pioneer in the industry and can be credited with introducing the rear-view mirror to the public. Marmon automobiles became respected vehicles, and by the 1930s, owning one was like owning a Packard or Pierce Arrow—Marmons were that good!

Marmon became a casualty of the Depression and stopped building cars in the early 1930s. Around 1931, Walter C. Marmon and Arthur W. Herrington formed Marmon-Herrington, Incorporated in Indianapolis and started making all-wheel-drive vehicles for the military. From 1946 to 1955, they produced small transit buses for inner-city use.

It wasn't until the 1960s that truckers started to notice Marmon cab-overs, which were rather square in appearance. By the end of that decade, a conventional was available. Marmon prided itself on building custom-built cab-overs and conventionals, with each one taking more than 550 hours to produce. The company boasted that their trucks were "made to last, built to work, and a dream to drive."

In 1963, Marmon became a subsidiary of Space, Incorporated, and its plant was moved to Garland, Texas. It later became part of TIC United Corporation.

Although Marmon received some acclaim, especially in the southern United States, the company never secured a really strong network of dealers and showrooms; and because Marmons were not mass produced, they could not compete with the larger makers of Class 8 trucks. Sadly, the last Marmon rolled out of its Texas plant in 1997, thus marking the end of a truly hand-crafted Class 8 truck. Marmon's Garland factory, today, is at work producing Navistar International's mighty Paystar.

Because Marmon is no longer produced, wise collectors will be picking up existing models, as this truck will soon disappear from the trucking scene altogether.

There is a need for a custom-built truck like the Marmon in today's hurry-up world. Although some customs are still built today by manufacturers such as Western Star, the time and care that went into each Marmon truck make the Marmon stand as an example of old-fashioned craftsmanship, especially when compared to the rules of modern business, where quality sometimes takes a back seat to quantity. Perhaps a new company can be born out of the ashes of Marmon, as more and more truckers are getting tired of the predictable "chocolate, vanilla, and strawberry" selection that currently rolls off the assembly lines of many truck manufacturers.

**1969 Marmon**
*An early Marmon conventional is seen here at an Anaheim, California, truck show, circa 1969.*

**1988 Marmon**
*Westwood Building Materials of Lawndale, California, hauls building materials all over Southern California and as far as Las Vegas with this Marmon.*

**1990s Marmon**
*Tinsley Trucking of Lake Havasu, Arizona, pulls perishables in the West with this Marmon conventional.*

**1996 Marmon brochure**

**1990s Marmon**
*This Marmon was photographed at an Idaho truck stop. Marmon made trucks the old fashioned way—one at a time.*

**1990s Marmon**
*From Sheboygan, Wisconsin, comes this late-model Marmon, owned by Gary Herman and leased to Aarco, Incorporated of Wisconsin Dells, Wisconsin.*

# Peterbilt

## In a Class by Itself

*Above:* **1967 Peterbilt/Detroit Diesel brochure**

*Left:* **1998 Peterbilt 379**
*Dave Lindsey's Model 379 truck and trailer tanker is seen at a Chevron Oil facility in Montebello, California. The tank body and pull-trailer were made by the Weld-It Manufacturing Company of Commerce, California.*

eterbilt is relatively new to the trucking scene, as it officially got its start in 1939, while most of the makers of Class 8 trucks began tinkering with making bicycles or motor cars in the 1890s and early 1900s. However, the company has roots that go back to 1916, when Frank and William Fageol founded the Fageol Motors Company of Oakland, California. With the financial support of investor W. H. Bill, their trucks rolled off the assembly line as Bill-Bilt trucks.

The Fageols became victims of the Great Depression, and ultimately the company was taken over by T. A. Peterman, a logging entrepreneur from Tacoma, Washington. Peterman, like the founders of Kenworth, wanted a truck designed to haul logs and lumber from the forests of the Northwest. Peterman designed a truck to meet his needs, and liking the name Bill-Bilt, he hit on the name Peterbilt—thus began the story of one of the most famous trucks in Class 8 history. Peterman died in 1945 before realizing just how popular his truck would become, although he did see some three hundred trucks produced in California bearing the early rectangular version of his nameplate; the familiar red oval Peterbilt emblem would not appear until around 1950.

Like Kenworth, its future sister company, the Peterbilt Motors Company started becoming popular after World War II, especially with Western operators. It was a common sight to see these older "Petes" hauling logs, lumber, livestock, petroleum, produce, and freight on any Western highway. By 1946, 350 Peterbilt conventionals had been built.

In 1950, the first in a long line of cab-overs was introduced as the Model 350, a Peterbilt that sat quite high. By 1952, Peterbilt cab-overs were as common as their conventional counterparts, like the popular Model 351 conventional, which appeared in 1954. In 1959, a newly designed cab-over with a slightly curved four-piece windshield called the Model 352 replaced the older Bubblenose and was refined over the years until 1981, when the Model 362 came out, bearing a more contemporary one- or two-piece flat windshield.

Peterbilt became a division of Pacific Car and Foundry in 1958, and officially became sibling rivals with Kenworth, which was also owned by PACCAR. Peterbilt moved from Oakland to a new plant in Newark, California, in 1960, with funds from its parent company. For a long time, Peterbilt dealers could only be found west of the Rockies, with Denver being its most eastern dealer. However, as the 1960s commenced, Peterbilts became a common sight in the Midwest and the East.

In 1966, Peterbilt came out with a tilt-hood, which was offered as an option on its on-highway conventionals in order to compete with Kenworth. The butterfly hood, however, was still the choice of many truckers.

In the late 1960s, Peterbilt introduced the Model 359 wide-hood. It was only available as a tilting-hood, but nevertheless was an instant success. The Model 359 gave way to 1977's Model 379, which satisfied truckers who wanted the "large car" look with both a long and wide hood. Many fleets wanting to reduce driver turnover will order a Model 379 with all the bells and whistles just to keep their drivers happy.

Toward the end of the 1960s, California's stricter pollution laws, coupled with high labor costs, caused Peterbilt to make a move from California to a more truck-friendly state. In 1970, Peterbilt opened a new factory in Madison, Tennessee, and in 1980, another new plant was opened in Denton, Texas.

In 1988, the Model 372 cab-over, known by many as the "Winnebago," rolled out of the Denton factory, but it received a less than positive response—a lot of truckers said that this rig looked like their mother-in-law. It was discontinued a few years later, only to be replaced with its earlier model, the 362, which is still made today.

Other current models include the Model 378 conventional, which can come with a set-back front axle to allow for bigger payloads; the lightweight Model 385 conventional; the rugged Model 357, ideal for the construction industry; the smaller 330 conventional, built for city use; and the Model 320, which is Peterbilt's answer to the Mack MR, a popular truck for the refuse industry because of its low-entry cab. In 1999, Peterbilt unveiled the 387, which is sure to rival the Kenworth T-2000. Along with this variety of models, Peterbilt also offers a variety of options in drive-trains, suspension systems, cabs, and sleepers.

With the new millennium comes new challenges, and Peterbilt is poised to take them on with vigor and creativity.

**1940s Peterbilt**
*West Transportation of Oakland, California hauled steel across the state with this high-mount Peterbilt, circa 1948. Colors of the West trucks were light green and black.*

**1939 Peterbilt 120**
*A rare 1939 Pete is on display at an indoor truck show in Phoenix, Arizona, in 1998.*

**1940s Peterbilt advertisement**

**1940s Peterbilt brochure illustration**

**1950s Peterbilt 360**

*Valley Bulk, Incorporated operates near Victorville, California, with this early-1950s high-mount Pete. Fiberglass is not found on this tough truck, which is capable of hauling oversize loads like the one shown in this photo.*

**1953 Peterbilt**

*This Peterbilt oil field hauler was leased to J. H. Rose Truck Lines of Houston, Texas. The rig's sleeper, which was made in the 1940s, was so small that it almost felt as though you were laying in a casket.*

**1950s Peterbilt 350**

*J. K. Paul Alley of Vernon, California, hauled cattle with this 1950s Pete cab-over. Other trucks in the Paul Alley fleet included the Diamond T and Mack cab-overs of the 1950s. The company's trucks had red cabs and blue cattle boxes. This photo was taken in 1957.*

**1950s Peterbilt 356**
*Layton Trucking of Oakland, California, hauled flatbed items with this Bubblenose Peterbilt cab-over, circa 1954.*

**1957 Peterbilt**
*This Peterbilt is seen pulling for Navajo Freight Lines of Denver, Colorado. Prior to deregulation, the "Blue-Eyed Indian" was one of the largest LTL carriers in the West.*

**1950s Peterbilt 364**
*Edward B. Wolf Tank Lines of Torrance, California, pulled petroleum with this late-1950s Peterbilt tanker, which was once a common sight out West.*

**1964 Peterbilt 351**

*The Peterbilt Model 351 shown here is one of several in the fleet of 1964 and 1966 Peterbilts owned by J. S. Schirm, Jr., doing business as Arrowhead Lines of Santa Fe Springs, California.*

**1966 Peterbilt 352**

*This Peterbilt Model 352 had a tall drom box behind its cab. Randy Jordan, doing business as Rajor Leasing of South Gate, California, hauled for Mand Carpets and ran cross country with this cab-over.*

**1965 Peterbilt**

*Jim McCallum's Peterbilt with a Mercury walk-in sleeper can be seen in this 1966 photo. Jim pulled for Mutual Citrus Products (MCP) of Anaheim, California, running through both California and Arizona with this tractor.*

**1966 Peterbilt 351**

*Photographed in Tucson, Arizona, in 1967, a two-tone blue Peterbilt Model 351 is seen pulling for the ATA Marketing Co-op of Fort Worth, Texas.*

**1966 Peterbilts**

*A group of new Peterbilts are seen at Motor Truck Distributors, the Los Angeles Peterbilt dealer. These tractors were set up to pull doubles, possibly bottom-dumps.*

### 1970s Peterbilt 352

*In order to compete with White-Freightliner, Peterbilt, like Kenworth, came out with this 110-inch (279-cm) sleeper cab-over. Peterbilt's, as well as Kenworth's, cab-over was an instant success for truckers who wanted quality sleep, and some of these rigs are still in service.*

### 1969 Peterbilt 359

*Steve Saucedo of Irwindale, California, runs this extended-hood Model 359 transfer-dump from as far north as Sacramento, California, to Las Vegas, Nevada. The dump boxes are made by the Superior Manufacturing Company of Ontario, California.*

**1970s Peterbilt brochure**

**1970s Peterbilt**

*This Pete cab-over has a penthouse sleeper above the cab and a drom box to haul more furniture.*

**1989 Peterbilt 372**

*By 1989, Peterbilt introduced the Model 372, called the "Winnebago" by many in trucking. Although its appearance looked aerodynamic, the truck never really caught on and was soon phased out of production.*

**1993 Peterbilt 362**

*Maggini Hay Company of Riverdale, California, had this Peterbilt in Blythe, California, when this photograph was taken in 1998. The Model 362 is a popular truck for hay and alfalfa haulers.*

**2000 Peterbilt 387**
*The Peterbilt Model 387 could pass as a twin to the Kenworth T-2000. This is Peterbilt's latest entry in the cross-country market, and only time will tell if this truck is a hit with truckers.*

**1990s Peterbilt 385**
*John Anker of Ontario, California, hauls cattle with this Model 385 Peterbilt truck and trailer. Conventional truck and trailer livestock rigs were once a common sight in the West in the 1930s through the early 1950s, but it's a rare sight when a newer Pete conventional like this one comes into the picture.*

**1990s Peterbilt 379**
*This Model 379 Pete, circa 1996, is based in St. Catherines, Ontario, Canada, and runs "the lower forty-eight," going as far west as Nevada.*

# CHAPTER 15

# Sterling

## Born Again and Going Strong

*Above:* **1940s Sterling brochure**

*Left:* **1999 Sterling**
*A&R Fimbres of Apple Valley, California, pull a set of J&L powder trains with their Sterling. The new Sterlings still retain the "Ford look," but in time, this truck will take on its own unique design.*

Today's Sterling is in no way related to the original Sterling, famous for its motorcycle-type front fenders, oak-lined frames, and use of chain-drive, but since the old and the new share the same name, this chapter will include both trucks.

The original Sterling company was born in West Allis, Wisconsin, in 1907 and was first known as the Sternberg Manufacturing Company, after its founder William M. Sternberg. The name was changed to Sterling Motor Truck Company around 1914, the start of World War I.

Sterling was there, along with the rest of the American truck makers, supplying the military with trucks during the war years. Building "Liberty" Class B 3- to 5-ton (2.7- to 4.5-t) trucks, Sterling became famous for its durability in Europe.

In the 1920s, Sterling's 5- to 7-ton (4.5- to 6.4-t) models became more and more popular, partly due to their well-known chain-drives, which provided better traction. So successful was Sterling that, in 1928, they merged with the Corbitt Truck Company of Henderson, North Carolina. While Sterling served as the parent company to Corbitt, both operated independently from each other.

By the 1930s, Sterling was becoming a favorite both in the Midwest and on the Pacific Coast. It was in 1932 that the company first offered a Cummins diesel engine as an option. That same year, Sterling bought out the LaFrance-Republic Sales Corporation, a truck maker from Alma, Michigan.

Most of Sterling's trucks of the 1940s went to assist the U.S. Navy during World War II, in the form of heavy-duty wreckers and heavy haulers of military equipment. In the 1940s, after the war, Sterling's popularity continued to grow on both coasts of the United States with models like the RWS-160H and the HD-115H.

In June 1951, the White Motor Company took over Sterling, and its nameplate was changed to Sterling-White. The year 1953 marked the end of this once proud truck, as White felt that Sterling and Autocar, another one of its acquisitions, were too similar, and Sterling was dropped from production.

The new Sterling Truck Corporation was born in 1998, as a result of its parent company, Freightliner, taking over Ford's Class 8 truck production. This explains why recent models of the new Sterling retain the "Ford look" of the 1990s.

The new nameplate is based in Willoughby, Ohio, not too far from Cleveland, where the White Motor Corporation phased out the classic Sterling. The new Sterling is aimed at vocational markets, in addition to truckers running cross-country. Whatever the application, Sterling offers a variety of different models, and with the backing of DaimlerChrysler, Sterling has the resources of one of the world's largest producers of commercial vehicles.

The new Sterlings are exciting—but the original Sterlings, which were tough, strong, and made no excuses, had a "John Wayne" character all their own!

The first Sternberg motor truck built in 1907.

### 1930s Sterling

*An early Sterling, circa 1933, is seen in this photo. Sterling was famous for its motorcycle-type front fenders, use of chain-drive, and oak-lined frames.*

> # Motor trucks are part of the life line of America.
>
> Sterling brochure, 1940s

### 1940s Sterling

*A beautifully restored Sterling is seen on display at a Washington State antique truck show. The Sterlings of the 1930s through the 1950s were sturdy and rugged—fiberglass and aluminum were not in Sterling's vocabulary.*

**1940s and 1950s Sterlings**
*Sitting in the old Lee Way Motor Freight yard in Nogales, Arizona, in 1981, are two old Sterlings that were once part of a fleet of petroleum haulers pulling for Cantlay and Tanzola Tank Lines of Los Angeles, California. Dick Taylor eventually bought them and put them to work in construction applications.*

**1950s Sterling**
*Photographed in Indio, California, in 1965, is a Sterling from the early '50s that worked for Imperial Truck Lines. Imperial was an LTL carrier in California until the 1970s, and its trucks wore the colors red, white, and black.*

**From a 1999 Sterling SilverStar brochure**

*Opposite page:* **1953 Sterling-White**
*This Sterling-White is the last of its breed, as it was produced in the company's final year of production. The new Sterling was introduced to the trucking industry in 1998, forty-five years after the original was put to rest.*

# Western Star

## Canadian Quality at Its Best

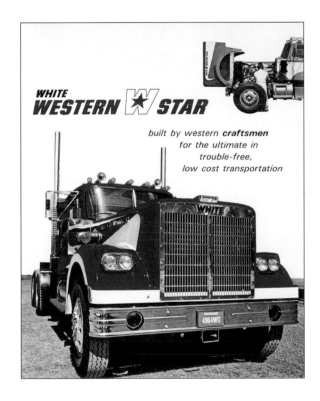

*Above:* **1970s White Western Star brochure**

*Left:* **1999 Western Star 4964**
*A Western Star Constellation Series, Model 4964, poses long enough to get its picture taken at a North Las Vegas truck stop.*

One of the newest contenders in the making of Class 8 trucks is the Canadian company, Western Star Trucks. Although Western Star is based in Kelowna, British Columbia, it was not always a full-blooded Canadian truck, as it got its start in 1967 as a subsidiary of the White Motor Company of Cleveland, Ohio. It is not uncommon to still see some of these early White Western Stars in operation. In 1981, Volvo took over White, and its Western Star division was sold to two Canadian resource companies.

Western Star trucks have been known for their reliability in construction, logging, mining, oil field services, and general hauling applications. At one time, Western Star was building both conventionals and cabovers, but in the 1980s, when making conventional trucks became the wave of the future and the demand for cab-overs subsided, Western Star stopped its production.

In 1996, Western Star introduced its new Constellation Series, using a newly designed cab. While its older cabs had looked just like the American Autocars of the 1950s through the 1980s, this cab featured a large two-piece windshield, more interior cab space, and a newly designed sleeper. In its brief existence, the Constellation has become popular with both Canadian and American truckers, as its clean, crisp lines and general good looks make this rig stand out from the rest of the pack.

Western Star is popular in other parts of the world as well, such as in Australia, New Zealand, and Indonesia, where the company's right-hand-drive vehicles fill a void left by most other North American truck manufacturers.

In 2000, Western Star became a part of Freightliner and continues to be the choice for both fleets and individual operators wanting something different, as the company offers hand-built, customized trucks to the specifications of their customers, with approximately 8,000 options available. Both the on-highway and off-highway models manufactured by Western Star provide an alternative for those who seek a truly different yet attractive truck.

**1960s Western Star**
*An early Western Star, circa 1967, from Surrey, British Columbia, is parked at a truck stop in Santa Maria, California. Notice that the name White is on the front, as Western Star was once part of the White Motor Company.*

**1970s Western Star**
*Parked at a truck stop in Big Cabin, Oklahoma, is a 1970s Western Star with a 1970s Kenworth cab-over as part of its load. While some truckers will swear that a Western Star is heavier than the rest of its competition, this claim is a myth.*

**1988 Western Star**
*"Mama's Wild Child" is a 1988 Western Star owned by Weymouth, Incorporated of Danvers and Ipswich, Massachusetts. This truck was the pride of the fleet and had just enough gingerbread to make it a good-looking rig.*

**1998 Western Star 5964**

*A slope-nose Constellation Series Western Star is shown here, pulling for Mercer Transportation of Louisville, Kentucky.*

**1990s Western Star**

*Why have a long wheelbase, an extended-hood, and a massive walk-in sleeper, when you can pull the sleeper in the form of a mobile home or house trailer like this Western Star is doing? This retired trucker tours Canada and the United States in style with his Western Star.*

**1988 Western Star**

*Taken in Massachusetts in 1988, this photo shows Gary Tinkham's Caterpillar-powered Western Star parked in his driveway next to a three-axle Fruehauf end-dump trailer.*

# White/ Volvo

## *The Perfect Marriage*

***Above:* 1942 White advertisement**

***Left:* 1980s White**
*This clean White stops long enough to get its picture taken at a truck show in Anaheim, California. Presto Food Products of Los Angeles took special pride in this tractor-trailer combination.*

When Volvo and White joined together, they also brought with them the nameplates of GMC and Autocar, and indirectly Diamond T and Reo, to form a "New Family" of trucks and a new company full of future promise.

White trucks can be traced back to 1859, when Thomas Howard White began making sewing machines in Templeton, Massachusetts. While in most of the years prior to World War I the White Motor Company manufactured steam-powered cars, it went to the more popular gasoline-driven engines by 1911. With World War I in full swing soon after this, White served as the U.S. Army's standard truck provider, building more than 18,000 trucks of many different types that saw action in Europe. After this conflict, White devoted itself to making mostly trucks and buses.

By the early 1930s, White had eased itself into the Class 8 truck market by building three-axle trucks, had taken over the operations of the Indiana Truck Company of Marion, Indiana, and would soon move its base of operations to Cleveland, Ohio. White was making inroads into the cab-over field as early as 1934, but in 1938 scored a hit with its Super Power generation of trucks and truck engines, which remained popular well into the 1950s. These trucks were well received by the leading van storage companies of that era, as their design made turning and parking in congested areas much easier.

While in the early 1940s White mainly concentrated on making trucks for service in World War II, they also came out with the WA Model at the beginning of the decade. The WB Model was introduced after the war, and in 1949 was replaced by the WC Model. The WC was available with either a gasoline- or diesel-powered engine and the option of an integral sleeper, which, although cramped, helped the WC become the truck of choice for cross-country van lines and chicken haulers in the Southeast.

The year 1949 saw the birth of yet another model, the 3000. This cab-over looked like no other truck ever made; it had a one-piece flat windshield and a rounded cab that was quite aerodynamic for that time period, which made it look like something from another planet. With an integral sleeper, the 3000 Model, like the WC Model, became a favorite for furniture haulers running Interstate. The truck came with either a gasoline or a diesel engine and was said to be more driver-friendly than the W Models before it.

In 1951, White took over both Autocar and Sterling, and in 1957, Reo became part of the White family. The following year, White bought out Diamond T, and the name Diamond-Reo came into being.

In 1959, the White 5000 came out and was made until 1962. It had a two-piece wraparound windshield and a fiberglass cab. To say that this truck was ugly would be too kind—it was definitely different!

Following the production of the 5000 Series, White brought out a more attractive truck in the 7000 Series, which was often referred to as the "Japanese Freightliner" by truckers in the 1960s, due to a slight resemblance to the White-Freightliner of that era. The company's conventionals of the '60s came as either the 4000 or the 9000 Series, and the famous Autocar cabs of the '50s were chosen for these conventionals.

The Road Commander came out in 1972 and by 1975 had become more refined as the Road Commander 2. That year, the company moved from Cleveland to a new factory in New River Valley, Virginia, which was joined by yet another new plant in Orrville, Ohio. The Road Commander 2 was followed by the Road Expeditor in 1976, the Road Boss 2 in 1977, and the Autocar Construcktor 2 in 1978.

The family was growing and all was going well for White until 1980 rolled in. Soon this corporate giant found itself in serious financial trouble, but Volvo came to the rescue.

Volvo had its start in Sweden in 1928 and provided the country with its national car. During the 1930s and into the 1940s, Volvo made several different sizes of both cars and trucks. By the late '40s, Volvo was able to manufacture bigger and more powerful trucks, as diesel engines were becoming more available and were offered in their 1946 truck models.

In the 1950s, Volvo was making larger trucks using their own engines, and in 1954, a turbocharger boosted up horse-power to 195. In 1963, Volvo came out with a 7½-ton (6.8-t) model that had air and exhaust brakes. Volvo continued making advances into the Class 8 market in Europe, and in 1975 made a truck called the "Middle East Special," which boasted both a cooking and washing area inside its sleeper.

It was in August 1981 that Volvo Trucks North America and the White Motor Company joined forces in Greensboro, North Carolina, to form the Volvo-White Truck Corporation and produce a New Family of trucks. Volvo-White's name was changed to the Volvo GM Heavy Truck Corporation, after GMC Class 8 trucks joined their ranks in 1987. The conglomerate is currently one of the largest truck makers in the world, with dealerships and facilities around the globe and trucks running down countless highways.

**1937 White advertisement**

**1953 White 3022**
*A perfectly restored 1953 White is photographed here at an Oregon truck show. The White Motor Company's 3000 Series was most popular in the 1950s.*

1947 White advertisements

**1950s White W**
*This 1965 photo shows a White truck pulling a straight-deck Wilson livestock trailer for Lynn Keirnes Trucking, a Colorado cattle hauler.*

**1949 White brochure**

**1950s White**
*A White with an integral sleeper is seen in this 1965 photograph; it was trip-leased to Motor Dispatch, an Illinois-based trucking company.*

**1956 White brochure**

**1960s White 5000**

*From Brooklyn, New York, comes this 5000 Series White, circa 1961. This rig carried Latin food products in the East and Midwest in the '60s.*

**1960s White 4000**

*A 4000 Series White, circa 1969, is seen here in Puerto Rico. Notice that the cab is the same as the one used by Autocar. This photo was taken in 1986.*

**1960s White**

*Another Puerto Rican White, circa 1969, features the Autocar cab. Dina, Western Star, Diamond T, and Diamond Reo all used this cab.*

**1960s White brochure**

**1966 White 7000**

*Ed Street leased his new White 7000 Series truck, referred to by many truckers as the "Japanese Freightliner," to Republic Van Lines of Los Angeles. The rig is pulling a drop-deck 40-foot (12.2-m) trailer, produced by the Dorsey Trailer Manufacturing Company of Elba, Alabama.*

**1970s White Road Boss**

*A White Road Boss, circa 1974, is seen here in Las Vegas in the early 1990s. The Road Boss was made for just a few years before being discontinued, but there are still a few being used today.*

**1985 White**
Some new White cab-overs sit in the Los Angeles dealer's lot on Washington Boulevard. These tractors were set up for local use, as they do not have sleepers on them.

**1980s White**
Kentucky–Los Angeles Express of Bowling Green, Kentucky, ran this black-beauty White, circa 1986, with an integral sleeper to the West Coast in the '80s and '90s. This photo was taken at a trucker's motel in Pico Rivera, California.

**It's a pleasure to drive, but make no mistake, this truck is all business.**
Volvo brochure, 1997

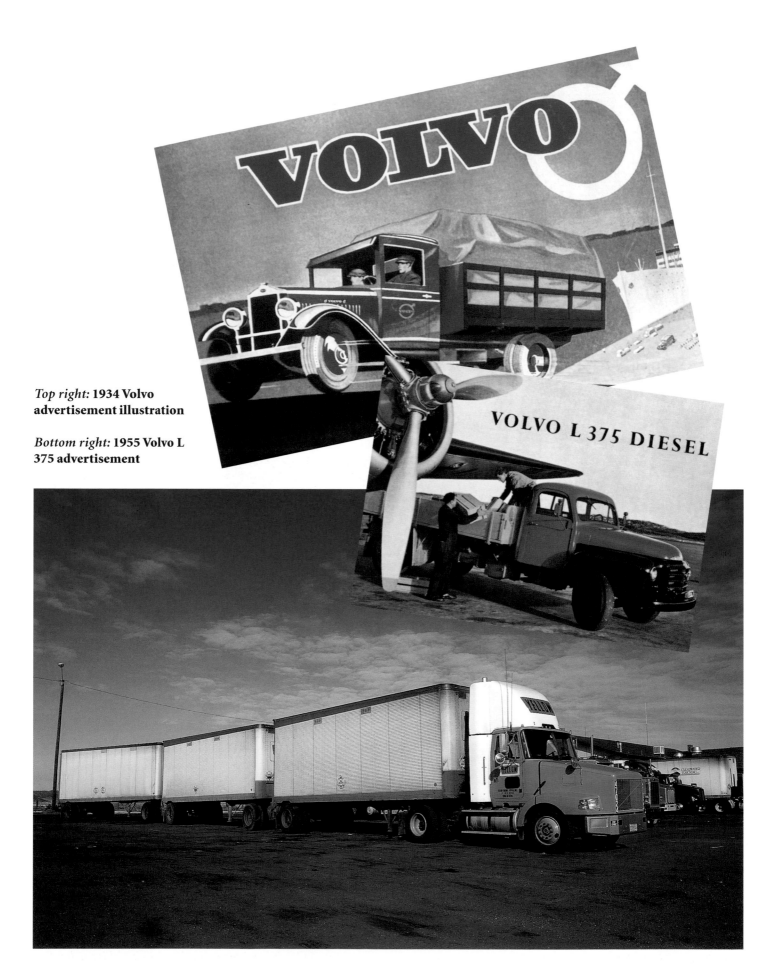

*Top right:* **1934 Volvo advertisement illustration**

*Bottom right:* **1955 Volvo L 375 advertisement**

**1990s Volvo-White**

*This Volvo-White is hooked to a set of triples. When Yellow Freight System took over the operations of Watson Brothers of Omaha, Nebraska, all of the Watson trucks were painted this color and became quite a sight to see.*

**1990s Volvo-White**
*This truck, pulling for American Way Van Lines of Waldorf, Maryland, is shown outside of a Las Vegas truck plaza.*

**1980s Volvo F-16**
*The cab and large, one-piece windshield on this F-16 Volvo, circa 1987, reflect the typical look of European trucks. This cab closely resembles the Mack Mid-liners of the 1980s.*

**1999 Volvo**
*This late-model Volvo is seen at Rip Griffin's Truck Stop in Barstow, California. The truck ran into bad weather in Wyoming, as can be seen by the vehicles on the lower deck of this car-hauling trailer.*

# Other American Makes

**1974 Hendrickson**
*This Hendrickson is owned by Dave "The Slave" Ward of Competitive Crane Rentals in Sylmar, California. It is powered by a 318-hp Detroit Diesel engine. The crane has been specially designed for use in the entertainment industry, where camera crews have to be lifted high in the air to film major motion pictures and TV commercials.*

## American Coleman

Although the American Coleman Company was formed in 1923 by G. L. Coleman in Omaha, Nebraska, truck production did not start until 1925 when they moved to Littleton, Colorado. Prior to the move, the company had focused on making snow-removal equipment and other apparatus.

The first trucks offered by Coleman were 4x4 and 6x6 load carriers that were popular with the military and various state highway departments, but a variety of trucks were produced over the course of the company's history. In 1928, they were making units for both the logging and oil industries for off-highway applications. In the 1930s, Coleman was one of the first truck makers to offer an aircraft refueling truck; many other manufacturers would later follow Coleman's lead in this specialized area. In 1936, Coleman offered a spectrum of trucks that were capable of hauling loads from 2 to 10 tons (1.8–9.1 t).

A serious labor dispute brought all of Coleman's production to a grinding halt from 1949 to 1950, resulting in a loss of approximately 350 skilled workers, as well as many dealers and loyal customers.

In 1952, however, Coleman landed a 9½-million-dollar contract to build Mule tractors, short vehicles used to tow aircraft, for the U.S. Air Force. This piece of equipment had a twin cab, four-wheel drive, and steering powered by a Buda six-cylinder engine. This contract helped get Coleman back on their feet, and the company went on to build 1968's aerodynamic Space Star, which was powered by an 8V-71 Detroit Diesel engine and could top out at 80 mph (128.8 kph).

## Biederman

Charles Biederman started building trucks in 1920, when many of his rivals were already established. However, in 1921, the Biederman Motors Corporation of Cincinnati, Ohio, was one of the earliest truck manufacturers to offer a six-cylinder gasoline engine; it was a Continental built to Mr. Biederman's own standards. As the 1930s rolled in, Biederman was making much larger trucks and in 1936 offered one that could haul 7 ½ tons (6.8 t), using a stronger Continental engine.

While Biederman was already building trucks for the military prior to World War II, it was during the war that the company built more trucks than any other time period in its history. The use of diesel engines started to become more popular in this era; Cummins and Detroit Diesels slowly replaced the popular Continental and Hercules gasoline engines that had powered Biederman's various models, which included a tilting-cab COE, snow removal equipment, fire apparatus, and bus chassis. Biederman was building wreckers and crane carriers for the military as well, and many saw civilian use after the war.

In the years following the end of the war, Biederman sold as many trucks as its small factory could make, but sales took a hit in the early 1950s, and annual production almost ground to a halt. Biederman ultimately closed its doors in 1955, but a few of the company's rigs are still in use.

## Brown

The original Browns were custom built in 1939 by the Brown Truck and Equipment Company in Charlotte, North Carolina, exclusively for a specific trucking outfit, Horton Truck Lines, much in the same way that Freightliner got its start. Designed by Horton's chief engineer, J. L. Brown, the first Browns were rugged as well as good looking and came with Continental engines.

In 1942, Buddy Horton, founder and president of Horton Truck Lines, merged his company with six others to form Associated Transport of New York City. The new company was greeted by an improved Brown, Model 513, after WWII. The 1948 Model 513 sold for $4,450, which was then considered quite an expense.

Browns were made available for others in trucking to buy after the war, and Cummins diesels became the engine of choice. Although the rigs were a common sight in the South, they were not a really popular truck and only about one thousand were produced.

In 1952, management at Associated decided that it would be cheaper and more practical to switch to mass-produced trucks like the ones that were offered by their competition, and by 1953, the last bunch of Browns had rolled out of the plant.

# Cook Brothers

The Cook Brothers started making trucks in the Los Angeles area at the end of the World War II. In 1950, Cook Brothers, Incorporated officially came out with its own truck, which was aimed primarily at the construction industry and those hauling building materials.

Several of the early Cook Brothers rigs resembled the 1950 Ford cabs, with an incorporation of some Reo styling, and borrowed ideas from the sheet metal of other truck producers in the design of their own fenders, hoods, and radiators.

It was during the 1950s that Cook Brothers began producing cement mixers as well as half-cabs that were to be used as crane carriers. Both gasoline and diesel engines were offered in their chain-driven models. Cook Brothers was one of the last truck makers to offer chain drive, even into the 1960s.

In 1958, Cook Brothers was bought out by the Challenge Manufacturing Company of Los Angeles, which was a successful maker of cement and ready-mix concrete mixers. Although Challenge initially continued to offer Cook Brothers chassis on their mixers, Challenge eventually began to phase out Cook chassis and use other well-known trucks as cement mixers. The last Cook Brothers truck was made around 1964.

# Crane Carrier Company

The Crane Carrier Company got its start in 1946, when three former servicemen started the Zeligson Truck and Equipment Company, converting and rebuilding older military surplus trucks. In 1953, the Crane Carrier was established to make custom-built rigs for the construction industry. During the 1950s, Crane took over Hinderlitor Tool Company of Tulsa, Oklahoma, and bought out Available Truck Company of Chicago, Illinois, moving the Chicago facility to Tulsa. Later, the Maxi Corporation of Los Angeles was purchased and moved to Tulsa as well.

In the 1960s, most Cranes were produced to carry cranes of various sizes and weights, but the company also built quarry trucks and integral construction buses. Crane Carrier of Canada made trucks for hauling logs of up to 75-ton (68-t) capacities in addition to making crane carriers. Crane Carrier Corporation products also included half-cab cranes, cement mixers, roll-off container haulers, and low-entry trucks for the refuse industry, which the company still produces today.

# FWD

Otto Zachow and his brother-in-law, William Besserdich, founded the FWD (Four Wheel Drive) Corporation in Clintonville, Wisconsin, around 1912. Besserdich would later go on to form the Oshkosh Truck Corporation in Oshkosh, Wisconsin, with B. A. Mosling in 1917.

Primarily a car maker early on, in 1912, FWD sold the U.S. Army one of their vehicles, which the Army converted into a truck. They put the vehicle to the test, sending it on a 1,500-mile (2,414-km) journey over the most rugged of terrain. The FWD came out with flying colors, and thus became popular with the military overseas; 15,000 3-ton (2.7-t) Model Bs were made for the Army in World War I. At that time, FWD was the largest maker of four-wheel-drive trucks in the world. During the World War, FWD provided cab-overs with an open-cab design for the Army.

Many FWDs saw civilian use in road building and highway construction. Unlike most of its competition, FWD enjoyed success in specialty areas like snow-plowing, high construction, public utilities, logging operations, and oil field work as well. FWD was also known for building the unusual in firefighting equipment, and in 1963 bought the fire apparatus division of the Seagrave Corporation of Columbus, Ohio.

FWD continues to be successful, building front-drive or four-steer rigs as well as special cabs and sheet metal that most truck makers say are impossible to build. FWD is famous for these custom-made trucks, which are something that seem to be missing in the mass-produced world of today.

# Hendrickson

In 1900, Magnus Hendrickson built his first truck—a cab-over, chain-driven rig with solid rubber tires. The trucks made by the Hendrickson Manufacturing Company of Lyons, Illinois, were distinctive rigs from their very inception, as they were built for special needs like serving as hoists for stone-haulers and dump bodies for refuse trucks.

In 1933, the Hendrickson company got a contract from International Harvester to supply IH with all of the suspensions used in their tandem-drive trucks. During World War II, Hendrickson kept busy making suspensions for International at the rate of six hundred per week, and the company also began developing air suspension systems. In 1948, Hendrickson began producing suspension systems for other truck makers as well, and these suspensions continue to play a major role in their current business.

Hendrickson produced both conventionals and cab-overs and by the 1960s had expanded into building specialized cranes that were offered as cab-over, low-entry cab-over, or cab-forward models. Hendrickson made inroads into the production of airport ground-support trucks in the 1960s as well, including fuel tankers, plane-towing rigs, snowplows, and freight- and passenger-handling vehicles. The company has also made armor-plated vehicles used for hauling currency and precious metals.

Hendrickson has always built the unusual, and for this reason they have managed to stay in business while others have fallen by the wayside.

# Index

# About the Author

Stan Holtzman, a well-known photographer in the trucking community, fostered a love for big rigs at an early age. He started taking pictures of diesel trucks as a boy in 1954, riding the roads of Southern California on his bicycle with a Brownie 620 camera in hand. Stan began his adult life as a trucker himself, but a near-death experience in the 1960s made him rethink his career: At age 21, he was loading steel beams onto a flatbed truck when the crane operator accidentally dropped 3,000 pounds (1,362 kg) of the cargo on his head, tearing his scalp, severing his right ear, crushing his lungs and kidneys, and breaking his back in eight

places. After an almost two-year recovery, Stan decided to spend the rest of his days behind the lens of a camera rather than behind the wheel of a truck. He now travels all over the United States taking pictures of big rigs and has ridden along in most of the various makes, hauling everything from livestock to pieces of the London Bridge. Stan is a regular contributor to several magazines, including *RoadKing* and *10-4 Express*, and is the author of three other trucking books, *American Semi Trucks*, *Semi-Truck Color History*, and *Classic Semi Trucks.*